Penguin Books

the Bushies

ALLAN M. NIXON is a bushie. He was born in an old Victorian gold town and now lives at the base of a mountain range north of Melbourne, where he is renovating a property using old materials like bush stone and centuries-old timber. Known as 'The Uteman' as a result of his best-selling *Beaut Utes* series of books, Allan travels Australia writing, judging ute shows, and gathering material for future works. He has written for numerous newspapers and magazines, including *Outback* magazine. *The Bushies* is his eighteenth book.

Ford Australia sponsors Allan Nixon's 'Working for the Bush' campaign to raise awareness of two of his favourite charities – the Royal Flying Doctor Service and the youth suicide prevention program REACHOUT! This association has resulted in a wide range of activities across Australia, including the building of a special ute – the 'Mongrel' – which has become widely known.

Other Books by Allan M. Nixon:

BEAUT UTES 4

BEAUT UTES 3

JOKES FOR BLOKES

MORE BEAUT UTES

REAL MEN TALKING

BEAUT UTES CALENDAR 2000

BEAUT UTES

HUMPING BLUEY: *Swagmen of Australia*

POCKET POSITIVES: *A-Z of Inspirational Quotations*

STAND & DELIVER: *100 Australian Bushrangers*

SOMEWHERE IN FRANCE: *Sgt Roy Whitelaw, 1914-18*

THE SWAGMEN: *Survivors of the Great Depression*

THE GRINHAM REPORT: *A Family History*

100 AUSTRALIAN BUSHRANGERS: *1789-1901*

INGLEWOOD GOLD: *1859-1982*

MUDDY BOOTS: *Inglewood Football Club*

INGLEWOOD: *Gold Town of Early Victoria*

the Bushies

True Stories of Australian Country Characters

ALLAN M. NIXON, 'THE UTEMAN'

PENGUIN BOOKS

PENGUIN BOOKS

Published by the Penguin Group
Penguin Group (Australia)
250 Camberwell Road, Camberwell, Victoria 3124, Australia
(a division of Pearson Australia Group Pty Ltd)
Penguin Group (USA) Inc.
375 Hudson Street, New York, New York 10014, USA
Penguin Group (Canada)
90 Eglinton Avenue East, Suite 700, Toronto, ON M4P 2Y3, Canada
(a division of Pearson Penguin Canada Inc.)
Penguin Books Ltd
80 Strand, London WC2R 0RL, England
Penguin Ireland
25 St Stephen's Green, Dublin 2, Ireland
(a division of Penguin Books Ltd)
Penguin Books India Pvt Ltd
11, Community Centre, Panchsheel Park, New Delhi – 110 017, India
Penguin Group (NZ)
67 Apollo Drive, Rosedale, North Shore 0632, New Zealand
(a division of Pearson New Zealand Ltd)
Penguin Books (South Africa) (Pty) Ltd
24 Sturdee Avenue, Rosebank, Johannesburg 2196, South Africa

Penguin Books Ltd, Registered Offices: 80 Strand, London, WC2R 0RL, England

First published by Penguin Group (Australia), 2003

5 7 9 10 8 6 4

Cover and text design by Brad Maxwell, Penguin Design Studio, © Penguin Group (Australia)
Cover photograph © Wildlight
Typeset in 12.5/17.8 pt Aldus by Post Pre-press Group,
Brisbane, Queensland
Printed and bound in Australia by McPherson's Printing Group,
Maryborough, Victoria

National Library of Australia
Cataloguing-in-Publication data:

Nixon, Allan M., 1951– .
The bushies: true stories of Australian country characters.

ISBN 978 0 14 300248 2.

1. Country life – Australia. 2. Australia – Biography. I. Title.

994.040922

penguin.com.au

Dedicated to the memory
of my grandmother
Grace Marion Nixon (née Kennedy) 1900-1995
who taught me to learn something new every day
and to remember the good things of life

and for
Janette,
the other lady of my life

acknowledgements

Thanks to the people at my publishers, Penguin Books, who saw the value of the work: Bob Sessions, Ali Watts, Kay Ronai and Sarah Dawson. To the rest of the great team at Penguin my sincere thanks, especially designer Brad Maxwell, a bushie who was enthusiastic.

Thanks to Karen Masman, freelance editor, who worked with me independently on the inital outline and gave great advice and worked diligently as usual to help formulate the book. Many thanks to Peter Ascot, who worked on the final manuscript.

Thanks to Sally Harvey, personal assistant to Pro Hart, who went out of her way to assist in many ways. Ta, Sal.

Thanks to my major sponsors, Ford Australia, for their continued interest in my 'Working for the Bush' campaign. Thanks to Kevin Lillie, Damon Paul, Darren Holland, Brett Polites.

My deepest appreciation to everyone who agreed to be interviewed for the book – all of them inspirational – I won't forget any of you. To their families, who assisted in various ways, I also offer my thanks.

My special thanks to my long-term friends Gail and Warwick 'Mongrel' Gregory, who allowed me to use their backyard flat for a few days and convert it into 'The Writer's Retreat'. Their support at a difficult time in the final stages helped me greatly.

Thanks to Wayne J. Gear, photographer, for the photo on page 52. Some photos come from private albums and are self-evident: special thanks to those people who allowed access to their material. For the photographs I took, I used either a 1975 Canon 35mm with wide-angle lens, or a 2001 Canon 35mm with 28-300 lens. Film stock was Kodak Gold 100 or 200, using only natural light as much as possible.

If I have forgotten anyone, my apologies. And please let me know, so I can update in future editions.

contents

INTRODUCTION 1

A MAN BEHIND SLIM DUSTY JOE 'TRUMBY' DALEY 7

WOMBAT THE SWAGMAN MR McKINNON 21

HORSES & HOT RODS HELEN BLOMQUIST 37

PAINT BENEATH THE FINGERNAILS PRO HART, MBE 49

REAPING WHAT THEY SOW TOMMY, LORRAINE & SARAH McCORMACK 65

LIFE IN A TREEHOUSE BOB PRUDHOE 79

WESTERN GIRL DANNI SHOWERS 91

BUSH LEATHER SHARRON & GEORGE TAYLOR 105

THE PADDLEBOAT MAN KEVIN HUTCHINSON, OAM 117

'WHISTLE' SYD WILSON 133

BANJO MAKER LAURIE HARVEY 141

THE MOVING MAN JOE BOWEN 153

OUTBACK & BEYOND MARGARET STUCHBERY 165

NED KELLY'S MATE GARY DEAN 179

'MAN WHO PAINTS WITH FIRE' RON CLARKE 191

TANTANOOLA TRAVELLER ROBERT 'NED' HUNT 201

THREE WOMEN OF SUBSTANCE MAUREEN TIMSON,
MARY JOSEPHINE O'CONNELL, CECILIA O'CONNELL 209

ONE OF THE LAST BOHEMIANS BRUCE DAVIDSON 227

BIRDMAN OF HORSESHOE LAGOON MICK 'GRUMPY' BETSON 241

'JOHN' JOHN 251

GRANDMA'S KITCHEN GRACE NIXON 275

Beyond the Front Gate

They're out there.

They are in bush towns, on farms, some even hidden away from the eyes of the public. You can find them anywhere if you really take the time and go looking for them in any locality just about anywhere in Australia. Some are local identities, some famous even, while some just lead quiet lives doing their own thing, largely unrecognised.

There's something about country pubs. Just walk into the main bar, look for the oldest bloke that is sitting at the bar, or one that has 'that' look about him. It might be the huge beer, a big man, a special bush hat, sometimes he might be the loudest or funniest man in the bar. Often, though, he is the old bloke quietly sitting on a stool sipping his favourite ale, sometimes looking at the race guides, sometimes smoking a 'roll-yer-own ciggie'.

Nine times out of ten they have a nickname.

I like to sit next to the old bloke. Often he may be just looking into his beer and soaking up what's around him. Sometimes he won't talk until you do. Other drinkers just accept them as the old fella in the corner or on his favourite stool. He's often the best source of knowledge, lived there all or most of his life, knows everything and everyone right back to his childhood. You can learn more about their town, their history and even gossip in a quarter-hour yarning over a beer with one of the old locals than almost any other way. I call it great research.

From the banjo maker in the mountain country of far east Gippsland in Victoria, to a woman in a remote gold mine of Western Australia, to Broken Hill and other parts of New South Wales. Old men and women, young men and women. Doing their thing and allowing me into their world.

Beyond the front gate of the home lies their world, their retreat from the rest of us. Personal space, sacred land – and where the real person is and where the mask we put on outside the gate is removed.

I have been very privileged in that the people in these pages have allowed me beyond the front gate to share time with me and reveal a part of their lives. They have shared their homes, their dreams, their memories and their work.

I thank them one and all for allowing me to bring to readers a glimpse of what they are like – I offer this as my homage to them and know you will find some you'll admire, some you may ponder about and some you will be inspired by. With me, I was inspired by them all. They all share a common thread – they are the Bushies.

Some were born and bred in the country. Others chose to move there. Either way, what they now do 'out there' is worthy of detailing. I hope they, and you, think what is here captures the same quality of what I admired in them.

I was born in the bush, the son of a multi-generation grocer, into a family in the same town for 137 years. I've written much of country people over the 29 years since my first book was published in 1974. I've had a lot to do with many thousands of them over those years, interviewing them. I get to sit and talk with them and see some of their world.

Bushies sometimes know what tough times are, and survive them the best way they can. This book is all about bushies, those people who have made it their lives. There is something about the bush and the people who live there, something very special if you can call yourself a bushie.

Years ago I was living in New Zealand. My arm was in plaster after an accident. I was broke. In order to survive I used to pinch one bottle of milk each night from outside houses. I never pinched from the same household twice. I had some morals. I had a packet of cornflakes and that was how I lived for about a fortnight. Yes, I knew what it was like to be a battler. Some of the bushies here know what it is like to battle too.

In this selection of bushies, you may notice a common thread. They all in their own individual way 'had a go'. None of them can claim to be 'silver spooners' – born to wealth and circumstances. They just 'did their thing', their way. Some even fit the mould of ratbags, bursting with irreverence and nonconformism. Great people, ratbags!

Some were content just to stay put and 'close to home', with others continually wandering and being inspired by the world, particularly Australia. They are creative, they are workers, or they are just content that they are doing what they want. Most aren't wealthy, but have a wealthy life. They are individuals – they are the Bushies.

If you enjoy reading these stories of everyday Australians and know who you'd like to see in a future book on bushies, please write to me at PO Box 46, North Essendon, Vic. 3041 and it will be passed on. Include full details about the person and what it is that makes them special. Enclose a photo if at all possible and include the contact details (including their phone number), and if chosen they will get a visit from me. If you think YOU should be in the next book, don't be shy; I'd love to hear from you why you should have a chapter set aside for you. One criterion for all those in the next book is that they must live in the country, whether in town or on a property.

For now, though, I hope you enjoy this selection of great Australians chosen at random. These are a few of my heroes – from beyond the front gate – the Bushies.

Allan M. Nixon
The Uteman
August 2003

A Man Behind Slim Dusty

JOE 'TRUMBY' DALEY

'WHEN I WAS ABOUT 13 THE HEAD STOCKMAN TOOK A WHIP TO ME
AND I HAD HUGE WHIP MARKS ON ME FOR A LONG TIME.'

I'm sure that the late Australian country music legend Slim
Dusty would have been the first to acknowledge the people
who helped him with his career, and that he'd have been
happy to read a story of an old mate of his, Joe Daley, 75 years
old and now retired on the outskirts of an outback mining-
town. Slim recorded 'about fifty' of Joe Daley's songs. One
well-known one, 'Trumby', is still selling some thirty-odd
years after Joe wrote it.

Joe Daley is what legends are made of. Not a bad effort for
a bloke who left school at 11 and was sent to some of the
remote parts of the country. His life is what songs are made
of, and his experiences and the people he met have been
preserved. He recorded two EPs of his music, and has published two books. It is his poems and songs that he will be

remembered for. I feel privileged to have spent time with the man and to be able to write about his life.

We hit it off straight away – the minute I saw photos and statues of Henry Lawson in his home. We swapped feelings about 'our Henry' and we knew instantly we'd be mates.

There's no bullshit with Joe. He says what he thinks and is not too worried about throwing in plenty of swearing to add weight to his story. But I detected a soft man underneath the tough exterior. He let it slip he burst into tears when he saw his newborn son. In his poems you see a mind of tough spirit but also a man with a heart. He is getting frail now and says his health has been pretty bad for a few years. I noticed a large oxygen cylinder on the front verandah and another beside the couch in the lounge room where we shared time and a coffee.

How does he want to be remembered when he heads off to the last round-up? Simply, he describes himself as a bushman. He is the very epitome of the 'old' bush, when horses and a tough independent life was all he knew. 'Jack-of-all-trades and master of bloody none,' he says with a smile.

'The bushed is fucked now. Everything in the bush now is done with the turning of a key – helicopters, motorbikes and four-wheel drives. They frighten the hell out of cattle and rough-handle them. I liked the days when men on horses slowly drove the cattle and looked after them, fattened them up and at the end were sorry to see them go. We were gentle compared to now. We handled the cattle and did what we had to, but now they pen them in a steel race and they are thrown down hard. Nah, the old ways were better and the meat tasted better and the lifestyle is gone.'

When you sit in Joe Daley's lounge you are totally surrounded by what he loves – memories on every wall from floor to ceiling: saddles and stockwhips, boudourie ovens, Aboriginal artefacts, a poster of a Ned Kelly film, books all about the outback. Hand-carved sculptures of Henry Lawson and 'Banjo' Paterson by 'Talc Alf' from up the Strzlecki Track. There are paintings of horses and eagles and anything else that has some meaning for Joe. 'It's just all the stuff I love and what means something to us.' A saddle that belonged to his wife's father lies in the corner. He died of cancer not long back and a large framed photo sits amongst others on a side dresser opposite me. A handwritten note from Slim Dusty promising to 'slow down next year' is signed and framed and sits on top of a huge television set opposite Joe's couch.

A pair of spurs hangs off the wall with some other odds and sods. A large dusty shelf is covered with pieces of minerals, rocks and bush artefacts. He picks up a stone millions of years old to show me. It has an ancient sea-crab embedded in it. He says to excuse the dust.

Photos of Slim Dusty adorn the walls, as well as other earlier country music singers like Buddy Williams, Ray Kernaghan, Stan Coster, and Gordon Parsons. In pride of place above the mantle is a huge black and white pencil drawing of Slim. Another one drawn by his daughter is above the front door as you enter. The hallway is also lined from top to bottom with memories, mainly of his mate Slim.

On the walls of the lounge are many photos of his family. Family is very important to Joe. Photos include those of a previous marriage.

The phone rang. One of his daughters from down south was being released from hospital today with Joe's very first

grandchild. Joe had excitement in his voice. He was very proud. He was off that afternoon for a three-hour drive to see his new grandson. He had framed a new poem he'd written about the new boy to give his daughter.

Joe still sips his coffee from an enamelled tin cup. I wouldn't have expected an old bushie to drink from anything else. His worn and battered stockman hat with band around his forehead sits as it is. It's seen better days, but the one hanging in the hallway is much worse. Kaye, his wife, thought it time he got a better one, for when he goes down the street. Something in Joe's eye tells me that he'd still prefer the even older one. Old stuff has character.

His RM Williams boots on his feet have been around a while but are still in good nick. They have that special worn-in look on them. Soft and comfortable. His braces. The sign of an older man. I wonder if in time we'll even be able to buy them any more.

His hands have lost some strength since he's been crook. They shake a bit when he lifts something heavy. His chest is weakened from life itself. But he's entitled to slow down a bit. He's packed more into his life than most.

It's a comfortable older style home with new verandah right across the front. Solid, well built. A home filled with one man's memories and joy. A home with a wife who has shared over 30 years of that great life. He's had his ups and downs, but here is his final peace. Here is home.

'My dad was "Big Malaka" Jack Daley, bushman, athlete, stockman and teamster. He was an expert hand at working horse teams and donkey teams. He was a Cobb & Co coach driver between Broken Hill and Tibooburra. He also drove wool wagons too. He was a road excavator, government tank supervisor, and like all good bushmen could adapt to any job. He'd served in World War I in the Middle East, Gallipoli and in France and was knocked about pretty much like a lot of them were in the war. Dad used to tell me about the exciting things of his time in the bush.

'My dad's father was an Irishman and distantly related to Abraham Lincoln. His mother was a Maori. They all loved ballads, music and poetry. Dad could recite Lawson and Paterson and other poets' work.

'Mum's family came from Melbourne where her father was a coachbuilder who later became a cabinetmaker. Her family loved music and singing. In fact, an aunt sang with Dame Nellie Melba.

'I was born in Broken Hill in 1927, the second of five children. At the age of 11, I left school. I hated school and had finished grade six three times. A friend of my father's asked me what I was going to do when I left school and I said I wanted to go bush and be a drover. Anyway, to cut a long story short he told my father and it was agreed I should leave school. My mother was hysterical about it, she didn't want me to go, but Dad just told her I wanted to go and that was the end of it. Dad was a very tough man and had been a bushman all his life.

'I was sent to BoxHole Station (also known as Nundora at one stage) a Kidman-Reid station that carried about 35,000 head of cattle. It was about 150 miles west of Broken Hill. My father said to the bloke who was giving me work that if he laid a hand on me he would kill him. He then said to me he'd kill me if I walked in any man's shadow. In other words, stand up and be a man and take nothing from anyone.

'All I had was a blanket for a swag, short, patched school

pants, a pair of sandshoes, a straw hat and a broken comb. I was put into a stock camp of about 10 rough and hardened men. It was a tough start. For the first 18 months away from home, I wished I was back in school. I was put to work like a bronco horse.

'When I was about 13 the head stockman took a whip to me and I had huge whip marks on me for a long time. He had said to me to get on a horse. I refused because the other stockmen had told me that the horse had killed three men.

'When I refused, the head stockman said to get on it or he'd cut my throat. I took off but got caught trying to get underneath the stockyard rails. He then took the whip to me. He was a very cruel man and treated animals very badly too.'

The memories of the whipping and that man still remain very vivid in Joe's mind and his voice is still filled with pain and anger. 'It wasn't until years later when I was about 18 that I got my revenge. I gave him a real beating.

'I was to remain in the bush for over 50 years and have worked as a stockman, cattle drover, horse breaker, boundary rider, fencer, axeman, bush racing jockey, dogger, rabbit and kangaroo shooter and most other jobs associated with the bush. I also worked in town as a miner and storeman. I don't profess to be an expert, I am proud of my common-sense handyman capabilities. I've also worked on sheep stations around the Tibooburra district but sheep are crazy bloody things compared to cattle. I also worked for eight years on the Strzlecki Track as a plant operator working trucks, front-end loaders, graders and dozers. Once in a remote area we even found an old Cobb & Co coach eaten by white ants.'

Joe has had a career in the bush that spanned both many

years and many areas. He sheared sheep on stations like Coorker Wells, Redlan and Gnalta. At one stage he worked an eight-horse team for £3 and threepence a week, working from before dawn until after dark, camping in sandhills without even a tent.

He worked on stations south of Longreach in Queensland as a dam sinker. He drove mobs of up to 800 cattle from Boxhole Station to Coburn Trucking Yards, near Broken Hill, and from Norryilco to Bourke.

Joe worked on the Dog Fence in South Australia and later the Dingo Fence, as they call it in Queensland. Boundary riders all had 32 miles of fence to patrol and maintain. They had to keep the fence up to six feet six inches in height. Dust storms could bury them and leave them with less than two feet out of the ground sometimes. Sand all moved in a day or so during severe storms.

One of the best things he says is a 'bloody good stockhorse, one that's a good walker. That's the main thing – a good stock-horse. We'd often sit around the campfire telling yarns and often we'd carry on about who had the better horse.

'Over the years I've had many injuries. Broken arms, wrist, shoulder bones, and one of the worst was when I was galloping on a horse after a "micky" (young bull). It jumped over a large saltbush and a big hole on the other side and over it went and my horse ran straight into it and I was thrown head-first onto the ground. The horse got up and took off and all the young bull wanted was to kill me. It hit me a couple of times with its horns, ripped my shirt off and hit my shoulder. It was about 150 yards to the nearest tree and I only just made it. It frightened the living shit out of me.'

Joe showed me his hands and wrists, where all these years later arthritis had settled in. 'When you are young you think you are indestructible, but you pay for it in later life. Out in the bush miles from anywhere you had no medical attention and just had to put up with your injuries.

'The worst accident I had was when a horse I was galloping ran into a wire fence. I was thrown head-first into a tree. I was unconscious in hospital for ten days.

'I was treated pretty rough right from the start. As an 11-year-old in a camp of rough and tough men, I got a hard time. I nearly perished once because no one would give me drink.

'The bush makes a man of you. The good things were the bush itself, the wildlife, the cool breeze at the end of the day. You can do worse than work in the bush.

'Later years I left the Strzelecki and worked out at Moomba on the oil and gas fields for ten years. A lot different than the bush work.'

I'm Just Me

There's times that you condemn me, and describe me, never fret
Rough as guts; 'n' what you see is what you stand to get.
I don't care what people think, I was like this as a lad,
And I still knock about the same, like my dear departed Dad.

I've got no framed 'certificates', or shares held in the bank.
All I own's a pick 'n' shovel, and Joe's my only 'rank'.
I play the game 'fair dinkum', always fair and straight,
And I don't trust those fellas who claim to be my mate.

He's the one who takes you down, by crawling, there and back;
Spreading heaps of bullshit, and claiming it's a fact.
All I want is a friend or two, to yarn away a while;
Share a billy or a bottle, and also raise a smile.

You may criticise my nature, or these patches in my pants;
But I'm as proud as you are, and play by ear or 'chance'.
I don't envy 'reputations', or salute your 'pedigree'.
I face the world with credence, telling all that I'm just me.

Joe Daley

28 December 2001

Deefa, the little dog, is chained up inside the front gate where he has his kennel. 'Deefa. D for Dog. That's his name,' laughs Joe. 'He's a bit of a wanderer, he always comes home, but one day he mightn't, so I have to keep an eye on him,' Joe says as he stoops and sweeps the little mutt up and cradles him under one arm as I take some photos.

I commented on the beautiful old gumtree inside the ripple iron fence. 'Mmm, look at all the bark, it's just shed it all in one go,' he says, pointing to a huge pile of ribboned bark lying in the garden. 'Beautiful. Just like those salmon gums you see.' It was a lovely specimen.

And so the gate is closed behind him and I take some more shots. Joe doesn't know just how much I appreciate being allowed 'beyond the gate' and into his private life.

'Hang on a minute, will you?' he says as he turns and goes back inside. His mate Alan is sitting on the verandah as I put my camera and notes onto the seat of my ute parked out front. Joe once wrote of this home in a magazine article:

We settled on the edge of town. We can see the mulga-studded hills, gumtrees and saltbush. Scrubber kangaroo come into our front garden, and there's a pure white roo that we've seen around here, as well. The roos come within a hundred yards of us and then hop leisurely off to check out another scene. They're good to have around the place. We have our own little bush collection, so actually, we are still out in the bush in mind, spirit and memory.

Some years ago Joe published a book *I Leave You a Song* but it was out of print, and he informed me he was having a new book published soon. In 1985 and in 1997, Joe was a finalist for the writers' awards in Tamworth, and has been recognised for his contribution to Australian country music lyrics in the Hands of Fame in Tamworth, New South Wales and at Barmera, South Australia. Numerous other singers have recorded Joe's words, including Keith Jamieson, Bluey Francis, Gavin Arden, Bill Bedford and Jim Ayres to name a few.

Joe returns to the gate carrying something. 'Here, I'd like you to have this,' says Joe, thrusting one of Talc Alf's hand-carved statues into my hand. It is a stylised carving of a bird. It was as if Joe had handed me his personal stockwhip or saddle. I was thrilled. 'I'll treasure it, Joe,' was all I could say.

Our hands outstretched yet again and while his shaky hand might not have the strength it did on the droving tracks of old, I felt the warmth and the sincerity and the wisdom that only old gnarled workmen's hands have.

I headed off down the rough laneway knowing I'd met one of the old breed, one of the legends, an unsung hero of the Australian outback. A bushman. A real bloody bushman.

Postscript

I visited Joe again some time later and his new book, *The Tracks I Left Behind*, was now published. The song of the same name, written by Joe, was recorded on Slim Dusty's CD *Travelling Still, Always Will* in 2002.

As part of a foreword to Joe's new book, Slim Dusty wrote: 'Joe Daley has been a mate of mine from a long way back. I've recorded a lot of his writing over the years and look forward to recording a lot more of his dinki-di stories.

> Tall and battered and bandy
> From a life on the droving track
> This is the picture of Joe Daley
> An old mate from way back.'

Since he wrote those words, of course, Slim Dusty has died – on 19 September 2003, just as this book was about to go to press. Sadly for Joe Daley and for all of us, Slim won't be recording any more of Joe's yarns.

Slim Dusty and Joe Daley: 'true-blue' bushies who recorded our history in their own unique ways.

Wombat the Swagman

MR McKINNON
HE LIVED IN A GREAT MANSION — THE AUSTRALIAN BUSH

I write this at Easter 2002, sitting comfortably in my office upstairs overlooking the garden, surrounded by my personal treasures, those special items we collect as part of our lives. Everything here, including the building, has been paid for in cash. You'll understand why I mention that fact, later in this chapter.

Sitting beside me, however, is one of my old photo albums, and a folder containing some notes I wrote at Easter 1990. Different times. Far different times. Between February and August 1990 particularly, things went horribly wrong in my life.

Hanging up in the garage below is an old pair of boots — totally stuffed. Memories of other times and a man I won't forget. Memories of Mr McKinnon. Some just called him Robert, or 'Wombat the Swagman', but to me he was and is always Mr McKinnon.

I first met him in the eighties. I mentioned him in my book *The Swagmen*, where I wrote:

It was June 1984 in the Victorian country town of Bridgewater-on-the-Loddon. He was an old man, probably in his seventies, pushing an ancient bike loaded down with sugarbags full of his possessions. He wore an old hat and ragged coat and looked very much a man who had seen life to the full. He said he had pushed the bike from Melbourne and was headed for Inglewood just six kilometres further on. I had stopped to give him an orange to help him on his way and hoped to interview him and listen to his tales.

He looked at me with some suspicion and was very reticent, but politely answered a few questions. I could see he was feeling anxious and wanted to be on his way. I knew I had intruded on his privacy. When I asked if I could take his photograph it brought our meeting to an abrupt halt. I sadly watched him head down the bitumen but, unable to resist, took two photographs of his disappearing back. He can't be recognised from these – I'm sure he wouldn't have minded.

At Easter 1990 he was the man who came into my life again, but unlike the first time it would have a far greater impact on me. Sometimes in our lives, particularly in times of crisis, we are presented with a kind of mirror. Something happens or we meet someone and suddenly we see ourselves clearly for the first time. It can be a bit of a shock.

In him I could see that he was the reflection of what I could become. His life and my life sort of intertwined. I was there to help him, but it was at a time when I probably needed as much help myself.

Australia was having 'the recession we had to have', as

politician Paul Keating so bluntly put it. I was one of many going broke and in desperate times. I was fast going under financially, at a time when interest rates were soaring and work was diminishing. The company that employed my wife was closing its doors after 100 years of operation. The publisher I was working for also had gone broke. Soon both of our homes would be sold, along with almost all of our possessions, our new ute and much more. I was a broken man. Depression had a grip on me and my doctor said to me, 'You can only go lower in a box.'

Coincidentally, in the midst of this I was working at pulling together a television documentary-drama based on one of my books, *The Swagmen*. Actor Charles 'Bud' Tingwell agreed to be co-writer and director. The production was progressing well, and I had also managed to talk American actor Robert Mitchum into being involved in the project, as he had been a hobo during the Depression.

I had spoken on the phone to him at his home in America, and while I was negotiating and clinging to the hope it would all proceed, I was at the same time heading downhill fast. It was like being on a plane but with a Kamikaze as pilot. I managed to keep the production company interested in the project and we even managed to get some filming under way, before they too went broke eventually.

I was trying, but I was losing the battle fast. A series of seven events over seven months saw it all disappear.

In the middle of this period I met Robert McKinnon. I cannot tell his story without telling part of mine as he was and still is an important part of it all.

I was headed to Bendigo and spotted an old man pushing his

bike along the road on the outskirts of Kangaroo Flat. I knew it was the old man I'd seen years ago at Bridgewater. I turned the car around and drove back to meet him. We spoke briefly and I handed him a copy of my book on the swagmen, not telling him that he was actually in it. He was very much in a bad way, his ragged clothes almost falling off his body. I asked if I could come and have a cuppa with him one day and have a bit of a yarn.

He said he didn't have a home but lived in the bush, but yes I could call on him. He was agitated and I knew he wanted to go, so we shook hands and he plodded off pushing his laden bicycle. I couldn't help notice that his boots were all but falling apart – he was virtually walking on bare feet – and that the old black coat had almost rotted away on his back. His clothes were filthy and falling apart and he smelt terrible. He seemed in desperate times.

The next day I went to his 'home' and took him some meat, fruit, vegetables, biscuits and canned food. He had said he lived about a mile off the road in the bush, and I eventually located him. Part of the ironbark bushland had recently been burnt in a fire. He had chosen his home well, in a hidden gully, unseen until you were within about 30 yards of him. I was shocked to say the least. I expected to find an old tin humpy or shack, instead here he was beside a small dying fire with no warmth left in it, his 'home' was a length of rope tied between two trees, a piece of tattered canvas draped over it to keep the wind at bay. On the ground were some newspapers for a mattress with a couple of rotting blankets on top of them. The papers and the blankets had rotted together almost to become hard with dampness. That was his bed. This was his home.

A jam tin on the fire had some water in it. His drinking cup was a smaller jam tin. A third blackened one was empty. Scattered under bushes nearby were all his possessions, a few canvas bags with his personal items in them, no doubt. There was no sign of any food at all, until I noticed one boiled egg and one slice of hard and unbuttered bread. He said that was all he had to eat.

He was quiet but gradually I gained his confidence, and as we squatted beside that most miserable excuse for a fire I began to learn more about him. The previous day when I talked with him he was 'over 60' and later in conversation he said 'nearly 70'. This day, however, he said he had been born in 1910, and when I told him he was 80 he seemed very puzzled. He looked quietly and thoughtfully into the smoky ashes. A few small twigs and the ashes smoked and then the fire brightened with a little warmth.

Through the bush nearby I could see a bush hut made of a few sheets of roofing iron, probably some kids' bush play hut. I asked why didn't he use that to keep out of the weather. He said simply, 'It doesn't belong to me.'

He was born in Hong Kong, and his father had been the captain of a passenger ship. All he was telling me, I later learnt, was true.

He said he became a seaman himself in later years. He worked around Australia on coastal shipping. He ended his working days on the Melbourne Harbour Trust dredging shipping channels. He lived in a Salvation Army hostel for a long time and when he finished work 'a long time ago', he lived off his savings. He'd never had a pension.

Later enquiries revealed he had lived on and off in the bush for many years and travelled from camp to camp. I met people who had seen him. He had favourite spots all over the state of Victoria.

He said he had lived in the bush for the last eight years and now it was his permanent home. One suspects it was much longer. He used to push his bike from Melbourne to Ballarat, but he said it was too cold and wet there, and he liked Bendigo – it 'has a lot of sunshine'.

He thought he had pushed his bike between Melbourne and Bendigo – that's about 150km – at least eight times. He also used to go to Bridgewater and Inglewood and he had a 'good spot' at St Arnaud.

He said that now he didn't go very far. The camp he had set up was one he often used but he had a few camps around the Bendigo district. This spot was a favourite because there was a kangaroo that visited him each day. He hoped that no one would shoot it. It was a 'good friend'.

After a long talk, he asked me if I knew where he could get a cheap room in Bendigo. I could see he was in desperate need of help. He was too proud to insist on help, but I knew he wanted it. I said I'd help if he wanted me to. 'That'd be nice,' he said. He was pleased when I mentioned the Salvation Army men's hostel. He used to live in one in Melbourne, he repeated. A couple of days later when I was driving him into town he confided in me that his camp was 'a bit of a lonely place at times'.

I had talked with the Salvation Army about the old man and taken more food and a lot of clothing, bedding, etc. out to him. When I collected him from his camp I noticed he hadn't used any items, not even the sleeping bag. He did, however, use the warm pair of pants, and he liked the solid pair of shoes even though he still wanted to wear his old torn socks in preference to the new ones he'd been given. After another day of reassuring him, we finally got him into his new home, at the men's hostel.

The manager, Doug, and his wife Bev, treated him like they would their own father and they gradually won his confidence. He'd been fully dressed and cleaned up and he even emerged without his beard as he felt he couldn't go to the doctor unshaven. Within a week he had a medical card, his old-age pension papers were being processed, a doctor was attending to his needs and he had settled in.

He cooked his own breakfast and joined in for a hot dinner at night. The other residents I spoke with at the hostel, all much younger, thought he was a 'great old bloke' and manager Doug confirmed they all treated him well.

My time with the old man had a big impact. Others called him by his Christian name of Robert and meant no disrespect, but I always called him 'Mister'. I wanted him to know he was respected. Somehow I felt I could never call him anything else. At this point we never knew his other name of 'Wombat'.

He was slowly learning to have confidence in his fellow man again. He was now sleeping in a warm bed. He told me he liked living there with a good warm bed and nice meals.

When we took him back to his camp to collect a few items he wanted, he seemed much more relaxed in the car. As we talked and he looked around his camp, he said, 'It's a lonely camp really'. He was lost in silence, his own thoughts, and I didn't intrude, but then he quietly said, 'There's a tame kangaroo that visits me, you know. Every morning and every night. It's quite tame.' There was no doubt in my mind he thought quite a lot of his bush mate. I sensed he may have been lonely for his mate and wanted him near.

Over the next few months I saw my old mate often. Every day he would go window shopping in town and he became a familiar sight. Mostly I would just watch him from a distance and leave him to begin leading his own new life. He went quietly about his business, disturbing no one. He walked everywhere. The Salvation Army did some investigation and eventually found his family in Melbourne. Only a sister-in-law remained of his generation but a niece and nephews were overwhelmed to hear of him. They hadn't seen him for thirty-two years and thought he was probably dead.

We arranged a reunion, and all the families including their own young children came for lunch. He remembered his niece Margaret, who was just a little girl the last time he'd seen her. Now she was married with children of her own.

His family presented him with a lovely gold watch. It was an emotional time for all. The old man seemed a little embarrassed, confused and overwhelmed. He quietly said his thanks and soon went back to his room, and his thoughts. The families were pleased just to see him, and he made an impact on the very young ones. Now all these years later, I hope they remember him.

My own time with Mr McKinnon had made a big impact on me. I wrote many notes of our brief times together but somehow – although I didn't fully realise it then – there was a reason for my having such contact with this man.

He had been living five months in comfort. Something told me, though, he would head bush when the weather became warmer again. I found out that every morning he would ask to be able to go into the garage. He always wanted to check to see that his bicycle was safe and that it was still there. He had bought himself a few items including a new water billycan – a large one. We believe he was slowly making preparations and once the fine weather of September arrived, he would probably disappear quietly one day.

On 5 August 1990 a phone call from Doug, the manager of the Salvation Army men's hostel, informed me that my old swagman mate had died of a heart attack that morning. As we were the old man's guardians, arrangements had to be made. A mate of mine was manager of a funeral home so I arranged to see him the next day.

Amongst Mr McKinnon's belongings there was a full-page newspaper article about him, written some years earlier, referring to him as *Wombat the Swagman*. His bankbook confirmed he had only withdrawn $500 to live on over the previous two years. In the morning Doug, Bev and myself went to make the funeral arrangements. He had enough money to pay for his own funeral and we decided to send him off in decent style.

It was to be a traumatic day. We arranged everything. On the surface, I was calm and in control. For me, though, other emotions would come to the surface later.

Later that afternoon, I went to see the bone specialist as ordered previously by my local doctor. 'Yes, there's a problem,' he said. 'You are very young to have this bone disease.' I needed to know the worst possible outcome. He didn't mince his words, he laid it on the line and was very blunt. He said that if it got to my spine or pelvis, I would almost certainly end up in a wheelchair within five years.

He said he wanted more full skeletal x-rays from head to toe to investigate further. He'd assess how far it'd progressed and decide what to do next. Some of the options did not impress me. He had really hit me between the eyes and I felt shell-shocked.

I left the surgeon's office feeling I had been given a death sentence.

Three days later we had the funeral of Mr McKinnon. I was invited by his niece to write and read a tribute to the old man. I was proud to do so. His Salvation Army friends, some family members and myself gathered to say our goodbyes. I had only read a few of the paragraphs I'd written when I began to weep as I read. I had lost my old mate who I'd helped find peace in his last few months and I was sorry to see him go. But it was more than that. In him, I saw myself and I was afraid. Also behind the tears, and probably the greatest reason for them, was all my own emotional trauma in my life, culminating in the bone disease.

As I read the tribute to my old mate it was as if a door inside me opened and I let go a huge store of anger and pent-up emotional pain. No one there really knew the real reason except Doug. They say sometimes you have to 'break down' in order to finally 'break through'. That day was one of those significant days. 'Wombat' had touched the hearts of all of us present, and a few edited paragraphs from the tribute I wrote to him will show you how I felt:

... *Life has many hard roads to travel, and Robert McKinnon certainly saw his share. Yet there is something that stands out in his story when we look back on his life. Right until the end he possessed something that would make the world a better place if we all had more of those qualities — he was one of those unique Australians that authors such as Henry Lawson, 'Banjo' Paterson or C.J. Dennis would have written about.*

Robert McKinnon had dignity. He was a quiet man who did not want to be a burden to any of his fellow men. He did not interfere in other people's lives and treasured his own solitude and peace. He did not voice strong opinions on other people or expect anything for nothing. He had adapted to a lifestyle that suited him and made sure it did not impose on others. Through it all he had a quiet determination for his freedom and peace and he managed to overcome any difficulties that life could throw at him. He was a quiet achiever in his own way.

He was one of those unique Australians that are becoming a part of history. He roamed this country and lived in the bush. He had few possessions, yet his love of the bush was evident. He lived in a great mansion — the Australian bush — amongst the gumtrees and the gullies, with the birds and animals for company. He told me the best times of the day were at sunrise and sunset.

When talking of the bush camps he said simply 'it suits me'. He talked of 'his' kangaroo and hoped no one would hurt it. His thoughts were not for himself but for one of his bush mates.

There are plans that his ashes will be returned to his campsite in the bush and a small memorial will be erected there, so that all visitors to the bush will know of him in years to come.

If something is to be learnt from our experience with him, it should be that we need to take care of others. It is a sad reflection on our society to think that for many years no one bothered to ask him if he needed help. Occasionally people did give him food, but when I took the time to sit with him and talk, I learnt that he needed help. I hope that in future we all can remember to take the time to listen to others. I am pleased I did.

He was a unique man who triumphed for many years over adversity. He made a big impression on all our lives – and we are honoured to have known him. I mentioned earlier that authors write about such men – I hope these few lines say something:

> Out where the ironbarks ride the wind,
> the eucalypt is strong
> If by chance you pass his way –
> do not forget to linger
> There's water in the billy,
> in that quiet secluded spot
> He's spread his last swag,
> beneath the Southern Cross
> An Australian son is weary –
> he enjoys his long repose.

We placed his casket into the hearse. On top of the casket we placed the wreath of flowers that Bev had especially prepared from his last campsite – wattles, eucalypts, fern and bush wildflowers. As the hearse drove away from the group for cremation, I stood back alone and looked on in silence, wondering how long it would be before it was my turn. I knew with chilling clarity that I too could end up far from what I imagined.

I had been diagnosed with an incurable bone disease and

told by a doctor that I'd be in a wheelchair within five years. It was the final straw. All the many months leading up to this had resulted in total despair.

My wife had to move home to her parents in order to survive. The last night in our home I spent alone, lying on the floor of a totally empty house, lying next to the gas heater with both my dogs and covered only by a blanket. The house echoed, it was so empty. Just like me.

Soon it was all gone – everything.

Just like Wombat, I ended up living for a while in the bush, only I had my small caravan and my two dogs – but no power, little water, little food and no money. Later I would end up in hospital. It would be some time before I recovered. But I changed and I grew and put many childhood demons to rest, and slowly with help I emerged again to fight another day.

Now I look back on it as if that was a totally different person. Now I can see how much I went through and that it did help me break through. I appreciate what I had experienced made me a better writer. Mr McKinnon unwittingly had helped me. Some may have seen his life as a waste and maybe even his death as not important, but to me it was full of the most poignant meaning. Though he never knew it, he gave me a great gift – the chance to see a possible future self. 'There but for the grace of God go I', as the saying goes.

Well, that was twelve years ago and much water has flowed down the Murray since then. Life for me has moved on and I rebuilt and took steps forward and some back, but again always forward. Always looking forward no matter what. My motto – 'You only fail when you give up trying.' Life is good.

The bone disease is still there and as I write my arm is aching, but no, there's no wheelchair in my life. Whatever the future holds I will tackle it and hope many people remember men like Wombat, who gave more than he could ever know.

He was Mr McKinnon – an Australian bushie.

Horses & Hot Rods

HELEN BLOMQUIST
'WHENEVER I TAKE ON ANYTHING I DO IT AT 110 PER CENT.'

To say Helen Blomquist likes horsepower is a bit of an understatement. She likes horsepower of the four-legged kind as well as that found on wheels.

Motorbikes, go-karts, rally cars, and hot rods were very big in her life and she has also achieved in her love of horses, particularly the Andalusian breed. She is a breeder of horses that have been national and state champions, and one of her foals fetched the highest price paid for a part-bred one-day-old Andalusian foal.

She has sold them to every state of Australia, to New Zealand and now one of her horses is a member of the Kuwait Police Force. Helen is, to the best of her knowledge, also the only woman in Australia who does show displays of traditional Spanish *garrocha*, the art by which the Spanish on horseback

use long poles to test young bulls for their fighting ability in the bullring.

Born in 1955 at Yallourn, Victoria, she has an older sister Karin, 48, and a younger brother Ian, 40. Her father was an engineer with Australian Paper Mills, and she grew up at Broadford. 'We won't go into the trouble I got into,' she says.

Helen was always interested in horses, and at the age of 10 borrowed her friend's horse. The bridle broke and she ended up racing down the Hume Highway, and when her parents found out, they immediately banned her from riding.

'So I used to walk five kilometres to the riding school and didn't tell them. I worked mucking out stables, just so I could be near horses. I got caught, but I kept disappearing and stayed involved with horses.

'I bought my own horse on my twenty-first birthday. It was named Venus. I couldn't afford a saddle at the time, so I always rode bareback. I remember at one stage I had her on a property but had to take her away – she used to chase the nuns at Chadstone Convent,' says Helen with a laugh.

Helen attended business college in Melbourne for twelve months, before starting work at Lanes Motors in South Melbourne in 1972 for two years. She lived in a boarding house.

'Gee, let me try and remember all the places I've worked at, there's been a lot,' she says. 'After Lanes I worked in an advertising office, then doing auditing for an accountant, then I helped my sister with her fashion agency, then a packaging company, a mercantile (debt collection) company, then doing wages for CRT Transport, back to help my sister's business, a friendly society doing health insurance as a travelling rep.

Most of my working life has been spent in offices doing clerical work.'

Helen also likes horsepower of another sort. 'I spent over twelve months navigating in car rallies for Simon Murphy. We won the "Most Improved" trophy at one stage, probably because in my first rally I kept getting lost all the time. But I learnt. I also did hill climbs and go-karting for a bit of fun. I also loved trail-bikes and used to go through the Cobaws. I remember one funny incident where I ended up in the flowers at the side of the house. I always liked speed. Whenever I take anything on I do it at 110 per cent.'

One of Helen's passions came to fruition. She loved hot rods. First she bought a brown VW, and joined the VW Club of Victoria. It was there she met Cameron McFarlane, a truckie, and together they built a special VW. 'We ended up together for 10 years and we built a great VW over two years. It was Cam who taught me how to rub a car back. I'd always been interested in racing.'

In 1984 she won 'best first-year member'. She ended up as president of the club 1985–86, and bought a second VW, one that became well known. She was also president of the Magnets in 1989–90 – the hot rod and custom club where all members were women.

In the early 1990s Helen's wild chopped VW was often written about. The car with number plates SLIK 56 was often seen in articles and even on two-page colour posters in magazines like *Custom Rodder, Chrome & Flame, Street & Custom, Supercars, Cars With Grunt, Budget Build Ups* and *Australian VW Power,* and rated a cover story in a European magazine *Custo Mania.*

Most car restorations happen in garages with every known tool and bit of machinery available. Helen at the time lived in a tiny one-bedroom house in South Melbourne with no front yard and a 12 square foot backyard – and no garage. So they rebuilt it in the gutter out in the front street!

Helen would be the first to admit that Cam did much of the work, being more experienced, but she too got her hands well and truly dirty. Not one panel on the vehicle remained standard, Helen and Cam making sure this would be a one-of-a-kind VW. 'It was a project that sorta got out of hand,' she says.

Just to be different they reversed all the openings, including the doors (suicide doors they call them) and the front and rear bonnets, which opened opposite to how they normally would on a VW. Modified dash, new larger souped-up motor, shaved chrome, moulded front guards, different rear lights, new front headlight treatment – all part of the total rebuild that Helen and Cam did.

Just after they finished the project, the VW won first prize in Radical Custom at the Adelaide Hot Rod Show. It then went on to the Street Nationals in Canberra, and many hot-rod shows in various parts of the country, winning awards and great comments from people everywhere.

Their next project was announced as being a Ford Anglia with a 327 Chev motor as well as their 1958 Dodge Custom Royal. In one article Helen said all you need to complete a large project was 'an overdose of patience and a sense of humour'.

But it was always her horses that kept Helen coming back for more. She had won a memorial trophy for ten years in a row with four different horses.

'I'd always been doing something with horses and I loved the Adalusian breed. I saw this horse called Poderoso, and I said to the owner, "If you ever sell it, it must come to me". Twelve months later I said to him, "If I get it I'd take it to the top". Two years later, in 1994, I took Poderoso to become the Australian National Champion. I'd always just been a bush rider so I had to learn how to ride properly. And I didn't know how to handle a stallion.'

In 1998, Helen started her own horse stud – Caballeriza Stud. In 1999 the stud won the national Spanish Champion Mare award. She has been the state president of the Victorian Andalusian Horse Association 1998-2003. She married someone also interested in horses, but it just didn't work out and they ended up separating. 'We had no kids – my horses were my kids. We're still good friends; he helps with my horses.'

Casablanca was a great horse and she soon had fifteen horses in her stud. Helen is a light-framed woman and you'd wonder how she's even able to control these large and powerful horses, but it is second nature to her. Since 1998 she has bred and sold Andalusian horses to every state in Australia, New Zealand and even to Kuwait.

'I've put out about a dozen foals, and one was sold for the highest price ever paid for an Andalusian foal in Australia.' Beethovan won the State Champion Part-bred, and at the same show Campeon Rafael won State Champion Spanish – it was the first time that the same owner won both prizes. Rosaria II won State Championships under-saddle at four years. Helen broke her in when she was 3½.

'Two of my foals are now trained to do war re-enactment displays in Western Australia; there's three horses in Queensland,

New South Wales and South Australia that are doing dressage successfully. The horse I used originally for *garrocha*, Casablanca, is in New Zealand and is now breeding.

'A policeman in the Kuwait force came to Australia and bought a horse from me for his own personal horse to ride in the police force over there.

'All my horses are classified into the Spanish Breed Stud books here and in Spain. Now I only have two horses left, and am rebuilding the stud again.'

Her horse breeding has been for the dressage market and people love her horses. 'I did the horse show scene for a long time and travelled everywhere, until finally I got bored with it. Then I saw *garrocha*. Jane, a friend of mine in South Australia, gave me a videotape of horses doing *garrocha* in Spain. The tape was in Spanish, so I couldn't understand a thing, so I just watched what they did. I taught myself from that tape and watched it over and over. I worked out from the training tape. I just had to work it out, and there was a lot of trial and error.'

Garrocha is an ancient Spanish display of horsemen with long lances, normally part of working with cattle being trained for the bullfighting ring. To take part in bullfights, bulls need aggression and courage. The calf is separated from the herd and two riders carrying long poles give chase. Once the angry bull turns on its tormentors his future for the ring is assessed. The riders with the long *garrocha* poles are known as *garrochistas*. Today the Spanish are learning and teaching their horses *garrocha* skills without the bulls, which usually takes six years to complete. They are now used for entertaining in public performances. And it was these performance displays that interested Helen.

She is a determined, if not stubborn, independent woman, and she wasn't going to let anything stop her. Finally her South Australian friend dragged her into giving the first public display at the 2000 Bushing Festival. She was – and to her knowledge remains – the first and only female in Australia to do it, and no female in Spain does it.

Sadly, Helen's wonderful horse Jezabella died in tragic circumstances in March 2002. So heartbroken was Helen she walked away from horses and couldn't even look at them.

Late in 2002 she got involved again and she has now thrown herself back into it with a passion. I am the first person Helen has been able to talk to about it other than Ray, a friend who got her going again, and he is determined she will go to the top. He is even trying to get sponsorship for her to go to Spain. The loss of the horse is still very painful for Helen, and won't be discussed here. It was the loss of that beloved horse that could have seen her never ride again.

She believes one of the reasons she has been successful is because she 'got to read horses', and as I could see, she talks to them directly a great deal.

There's a new horse, a part-bred Andalusian, that keeps her busy. Jedda was the name given by Dawn, the barmaid of the local pub. Jedda is a four-year-old and Helen is excited at the results of working with the horse.

She just broke the horse in and on just the sixth ride Jedda walked into the main bar of the pub and interacted with the patrons. She now even will take a piece of apple off the top of a can of drink. She also likes a drink. Being in closed unfamiliar territory with people is strange for a horse, and one assumes she totally trusts Helen enough to do it.

Some few weeks later I returned to see Helen and Jedda at work and the horse is totally devoted to her and has come ahead in leaps and bounds. Helen showed me how the horse can do the waltz in the main bar of the pub with music playing in the background. 'She's shaping up to breaking in,' says Helen. 'She'll be soon doing *garrocha* and also line dancing.'

Line dancing? Yes, you read right. Helen has already been involved in a display of horses doing line dancing at the Tamworth Country Music Festival, and worked with horseman David Williams. 'I was his backup. The horse (Domero) he used at Tamworth is now in New Zealand – it is in the *Lord of the Rings* movie. Another horse I found at Woodend is in the second movie; I did the deal for them.'

Helen is involved in a *Mad Max* day. She is also working on a special idea – a horse in full armour doing a duel with a car. She plans for Jedda to become the star of many shows all over Australia. She and Ray are working on an act to take on tour. Ray is a country singer amongst other things, and they believe they are putting together something very special that audiences will like to see.

They want to travel the clubs, pubs, horse shows and other events, as well as see the country. 'I want to go travelling Australia, promoting the breed and having a good time,' she says. Seeing these two determined people, I'm sure they can and will do it well.

On my return to see Helen she showed me a video of another horse she had just bought. BHM Black Thunder is a magnif- icent black stallion, the son of Esplendido, a magnificent horse which Helen owned. Five-year-old Thunder already has a long list of awards to its name, including Australian Stallion and

Reserve Champion. Under Helen's training, this is a horse that will become very well known as it is to be Helen's main *garrocha* display horse. Jedda will also be backup for *garrocha*, but will do the main dancing displays.

A big goal for Helen now is to train with the *garrocha* training school in Spain. If anyone can do it, it will be Helen.

And by way of afterthought she informed me, 'Oh yeah, recently I spent $1000 to buy a VW Baja and I'd like to do it up to go dirt road racing.'

She has a definite philosophy wrapped up in a couple of lines: 'I go for something I've never done before and I like to try to achieve something no one else has.'

Paint Beneath the Fingernails

PRO HART, MBE
'I've just begun to paint.'

BROKEN HILL, NSW
17 FEBRUARY 2002

I couldn't find a park outside Pro Hart's Art Gallery as there were a few cars already there, so I moved slowly on a bit. As I backed into a spot I was right at the front gate of the house next door. I knew it was Pro's house; there was a Rolls-Royce in the carport. And I was sure because there was the man himself, standing on the lawn checking out my ute. He stood there in shorts, paint splattered T-shirt and sandals. It was the image I knew of Pro Hart.

I got out to go to the gallery, grabbing my camera as I hoped I might get a photo of him. I nodded and said g'day the same time Pro did. 'Like your ute, mate,' he says.

And that's how it all started. We ended up spending some time underneath a huge tree in the garden next to the carport, talking on his front lawn for a few minutes, and then unexpectedly he invited me in for a coffee. A couple of hours passed at the dining room table yarning over a couple of coffees – with his wife, mother-in-law, two grandchildren coming and going and two children, son John and daughter Marie, also coming and going. A missionary from New Guinea and his wife called in for a while and a coffee. I sensed this was a house where family and friends were important.

But then we went for a walk through Pro's world. Son John and I talked of the new Monaro car he's ordered, and Pro delighted in showing me one of his work areas and his interest in motoring – a couple of Rolls-Royces, a Bentley, a 1927 Chev and also some of his special interests in automotive mechanisms, his own inventions and more. Pro has a great dislike of oil companies and one invention is 'perfection zero-pollution emissions for engine'. We spent a lot of time talking of a wide variety of subjects as we wandered around one of the cluttered but enthralling studios, workshop, carport.

It's not easy to write a story about Pro Hart. He's complicated but he's a simple man. Complicated in that he's multifaceted, multi-talented, inquisitive, opinionated, interested and interesting, yet simple when queried. Ask him about what he remembers about his childhood and the answer comes back: 'boring'. Ask him his thoughts on the republic or the monarchy and you'll need an hour to listen to his views.

His mind is active; he darts from one subject to another with interest and passion. We talk of his God and how his life is in the hands of God. 'I don't worry about a lot of things; "he" will guide me. I just let it all happen,' he says.

We wander to the back of the shed to get some prints that he wants me to have and some to give to Tania Kernaghan.

I'd dropped her off at the airport and she missed seeing him. Pro was sorry he missed her; he knows her brother Lee and asked if I'd get some stuff to her. He handed me a couple of small New Testaments, the back cover painted with a Pro Hart original and signed. A little sticker on the inside cover reads: 'The painting on the cover of this book will one day turn to dust but the Word of God Lasts for Eternity. Pro Hart.'

We got into swap mode. He signs a handful of posters of his work and while he is looking for a book, I go to the ute to drop off the paintings and grab him a copy of my latest book. 'I'll read every word of it,' he says earnestly and immediately tries to find a book. He also signed copies of a poster of him standing next to a Rolls-Royce over which he painted the history of Australia for the millennium.

He hands me two copies of *The Undiscovered Pro Hart*. He signs them, one for Tania and one a pencilled drawing of my ute and his signature. I didn't ask, but Pro was generous and wanted me to have them. I got the better of the deal, but he generously didn't seem to mind one bit. I've since given him some more of my books – but somehow it seemed inadequate.

Pro is anti-republic. I am pro-republic. 'I don't say I don't like the idea, I don't know, but I didn't like the way and who was pushing the ideas, that's how I came to paint the history of Australia on that Rolls – to stick it up the republicans.'

I am a republican but I agreed with Pro that I believed the referendum failed because of some of the people involved and the public didn't want the model presented. I didn't tell him I was a republican. I expected that the next time we meet we'll have some more things to talk about.

We both are pro-guns and the right to own them. Pro has

taken his sport much further; he holds a pistol licence and has many guns locked away including a cannon.

We yarned about all sorts of stuff that Aussie blokes do in a shed – only Pro's shed is a bit different to the norm.

Anyone who knows Pro knows he holds a massive collection of artworks from all over the world. And we wander through this studio shed he was using at the time. The other one is being used by a daughter. Sheds are everywhere on Pro's property. One holds a fully equipped gymnasium. Pro introduces me to a bloke who is weight training. People come and go here, all friends of Pro's. Security keeps the unwanted away.

We to and fro our way from the shed to the carport, to studio to office and around the yard looking at Rollers, as he refers to his Rolls-Royces outside the gallery.

I got his already very fertile imagination ticking over as we stood and looked at a Rolls-Royce imagining it being cut down into a ute. 'So why don't you make one of these into a ute?' says I cheekily. 'It would be a marvellous-looking machine and you could have some fun with it, paint it up like the one you did on the history of Australia.'

Pro's creative mind was already imagining it. He pointed to the shiny Roller with a sweep of his arm. 'We could cut it through there,' he says. 'I got two seats in the front, I don't need the back ones – but gee it'd be a long shape,' he says.

'Nah, it'll be great,' says I excitedly. And I could tell he really wanted to do it. We talked of the style and discussed various aspects. I think that's why we got on so well, I treated him as an ordinary man and was not afraid to make an opinion. Either that or he was flabbergasted some stranger would have the nerve to tell him to get an angle grinder to work and wreck his Rolls. I believe in being honest and telling them what you think.

'I'm going to be in the bad books with your wife,' I said. We were looking at the vehicle she often drives. A nice Rolls with white leather seats. She'd already commented over coffee about not wanting it cut down. But something tells me Pro would soon find another one. We looked at the other one already painted up by Pro for the year 2000 on a theme of God Bless Australia.

He thought that might be a bit too good to cut up. But I could see he was seriously looking at it. 'The spiders love making nests on it,' he says as he wipes away a web on the body of the Rolls. All cars had some red Broken Hill dust on them, something that happens all the time, but it seemed very appropriate that Pro Hart's Rolls had red outback dust on them. Almost an unconscious mockery of those city Rolls-Royces of the silver-spooners.

I suggested I get back to him. I had an idea for another ute with the Pro touch. One that might save Mrs Hart from wishing the Uteman fella hadn't encouraged her husband to chop up a Rolls.

Pro fired up one of his motoring inventions and his scientific mind is as fertile as his artistic mind. His knowledge left me in awe within five minutes. His didn't worry about talking of art as he was much more enthralled to regale me with what was in the carport, his tinkering area (the real in-depth stuff was in another building where he has lathes and other machinery).

I wish I could give you a description of his inventive work but I can't and I wouldn't. There's enough rip-off merchants out there who would love to gain access to Pro's inventive

mind. I felt I had been graciously given an insight into another side of this famous man. He shared his 'other world' with me – and probably didn't need me to waste any more of his Sunday afternoon.

'No, that's fine. I can have Sunday off, and I'll get stuck into some work tonight anyway,' he said matter-of-factly. I met three of four dogs. John's two and one of Pro's. I could see an Alsatian through a window in the backyard.

We yarned on many subjects and he had no problems that I had my camera with me. He says he just doesn't like video cameras. He was relaxed. But still I felt I'd annoyed his 'day off' long enough. Finally, a half-hour later we shook hands again and said we'd yarn again one day. 'When are you leaving town?' he asked.

'Either tomorrow or Tuesday.' I was coming back the next morning to have a look through his gallery in more detail – you need time to see it all.

'Call in after you've been through the gallery and we'll have another coffee,' he says.

With that I left, knowing Pro was looking at the ute and listening to the exhaust as I headed off up the street. He had liked the amount of ground clearance of my one-off ute. He reckons a lot of people in the bush would like to have one. I reckon Pro Hart should have one parked next to one of the Rolls-Royces and add some of his unique style to it. He does a lot of work for charity, the Kidney Foundation in particular. I had my mind ticking over. I'll be back, Pro.

Monday morning and I'm back to go through the Pro Hart gallery. Pro spots me and I never make it, he's in the carport and we yarn again. And yes he agrees that cutting this Rolls-Royce down might not be the best. His wife would prefer not to. 'But I can pick up an old Rolls for about $20,000 so you never know.' He is still keen on the idea.

To cut a long story short Pro agreed to an idea I had and as he didn't have a ute it appealed. 'I like Fords actually. Those early ones had some real go in them.'

I remember when young my parents had a Pro Hart print in a plain white frame. It was one of those popular images that Pro is famous for – the stick-like figures of people at a local event in the bush. That was my introduction to Pro Hart. I knew he did art with cannons and other implements. I saw the ad on TV where he uses all sorts of stuff splashed over a carpet and the little Italian woman cleaner exclaims, 'Oh, Mr Hart!' If for nothing else he'd always be famous just for that TV ad. I knew he was just 'there' – a famous Australian painter who lived in Broken Hill.

My other visions of Pro before were his thick glasses, short stocky frame and being surrounded by Rolls-Royces. All of this is true of Pro, but there's a great deal more that the average person never sees.

Pro Hart is a bundle of energy. His mind seems to run at a great rate. He is known for dressing in shorts, thongs or sandals, T-shirt spattered in paint. It is his 'uniform', as much a part of Pro as the collection of Rolls-Royces parked in and around the buildings. Somehow I can't imagine him in anything else, it suits him. It is almost like him saying this is just me. This is who I am.

He is not what you'd expect of a multi-talented multi-millionaire known around the world. He is controversial but he has a couldn't-give-a-damn attitude. It is almost that he is mocking those who profess their own fame. He is well aware of his talent, however. He has been ripped off more than once and it was a subject we discussed in detail.

Now he can protect his work in that each painting has an embedded bar code, a silicon chip and a sample of Pro's own DNA. 'It cost a fortune to set up originally, we had it done in America but it's the only way to protect your work. Now we have it all set up. There's a heap of cheats out there.'

Protection comes with fame. He knows exactly how long it takes police to get to the property. There are three alarm systems at Pro's place, dogs and huge steel bars on the windows of the gallery where millions of dollars worth of his and many other painters' original works hang. He is an A grade pistol shooter, a life-member of the local pistol club. I suspect you'd be treading dangerous ground if you did anything on his property or within the family. But he seems unperturbed by it all. He puts his trust in a far greater thing than man.

His protruding belly highlights the paint-splattered polo shirt. He looks a strong man, particularly in his forearms. He is casual, but within minutes of meeting him you realise you are talking with a different man – an intelligent, informed man. And he does not always look straight at you. It is almost as if he looks off into a distance to gain and bring back his knowledge. His casualness does not quite hide his immense character, his opinions, his knowledge, his beliefs.

Pro is a Christian, but like the rest of his casualness, his belief in God just emerges almost unannounced within conversation. He hands out small *New Testaments* by the hundreds each year with a small Pro Hart painting on the back of each. 'I just hand everything over to the fella upstairs,' he says, explaining his Christian belief.

Pro and I got on like we'd known each other for years.

Pro Hart is working class. At 75, he is still working and he says he's only just begun. You know as soon as you talk art with him that he has a million ideas still not on canvas. The last page of the book *The Undiscovered Pro Hart* has his hand-written comment, 'I've just begun to paint.'

On another trip to Broken Hill I handed Pro a parcel. 'What's this?' he says. 'Well, I disturbed your Sunday, including your lunch, so here's something.' I had some flowers for his wife and mother-in-law. Mrs Hart's mother now lives in the local old folks home and comes for Sunday lunch.

'Aw gee, you shouldn't have, thanks, mate,' says Pro, opening a parcel of fresh yabbies. 'I'll have these for tea,' he says. Mrs Hart was putting the flowers into large vases. Pro then talks of the large yabbies of New Guinea. He forgot we already discussed them last trip, but it doesn't matter, Pro often repeats things and I always find him interesting.

Since then we've spent a bit of time together and I wouldn't go to Broken Hill without calling to see them. There has been one very important reason why I made numerous trips to see him in 2002.

When I left him the first time, he had agreed for me to try and pull something together. I told him of my idea with a ute and he liked it. I returned to Melbourne, determined to convince my major sponsors, Ford Australia, to give Pro a ute to paint in his unique style. Although it was met with some resistance by one of the bosses I was responsible to, another liked the idea and gave me the go-ahead to pursue it. To cut a long story short, I had pulled together in writing for Ford and with Pro's staff, a project that would raise some money for charity and see a one-of-a-kind Pro Hart ute. Pro would receive another ute for his efforts. Naturally Ford would get the publicity as well. I went back to see Pro and we settled on the details.

Then it was another trip, to supervise the unloading of a yet-to-be-released Falcon BA XR6 Turbo ute. The public hadn't yet seen it so I was in charge of making sure security was tight around this ute, even having Pro's carport totally wrapped in black plastic.

I had to get security documents signed by anyone who would be involved. Pat and Lindsay Wilkins at the local smash repair company would be doing the final sealing and heat-baking treatment of Pro's paint job and we had to get the ute into and out of their place without anyone seeing it. We moved it back to Pro's under the cover of darkness. I was determined that the project would be kept under wraps until a public launch.

The day it arrived at Pro's we didn't have to wait long for Pro to get to work. He had some paint on the vehicle within about half an hour after rubbing the brand new ute down with some special sandpaper. Lindsay was covering all the lights and other bits we didn't want painted with masking tape, but Pro was getting his creative juices flowing.

Over about the next ten days Broken Hill had some of the worst winds and dust storms that Pro could remember. He worked under some of the most trying conditions known, the black plastic flapping loudly day and night as he worked. It drove him nuts. But still he continued on, and as we had a brief for him to work to he knew what I wanted. I'd given him a list of subjects and themes I'd come up with and added to by the bosses at Ford. We agreed he had to have creative freedom, though.

I talked daily on the phone with Sally, Pro's personal assistant, and it was certain he would soon have it finished, so I packed and was off for another few days to Broken Hill. People wondered why I was going to the Hill so many times.

It was finished. He'd spent many, many hours on it and now it was ready. All we needed to do was a final baking in Lindsay and Pat's workshop. This was done and it was ready a few days later to be taken by truck to Melbourne. We loaded it and saw it off. The next day I too was off and finally back in Melbourne to meet the truck on arrival. We unloaded it in a secret location where I'd handed it over. It was moved later to another location, and the meetings began re the planned event.

Pro liked my suggestion of where the money would go when we auctioned off the ute, and so it was agreed that all money would go to the Royal Flying Doctors Service, with 50 per cent going to the Broken Hill base and the remainder to be split amongst the other sections of RFDS Australia wide.

I rang RFDS in Sydney and informed them what we were doing, they were thrilled, and I followed it up with an email. As I'd done other projects for RFDS they knew me as a long-term fundraiser. Though not complete until after 2002 – the Year of the Outback – the idea I had put to Ford and Pro was our contribution to the Year of the Outback.

We trust the auctioning of the Falcon BA XR6 Turbo ute will raise a great deal of money for the Flying Doctors. Someone is going to have an amazing one-of-a-kind ute to add to their collection. Pro says he would never again take on a project like it. This is the first and last ute he will ever paint.

Pro Hart is famous and knows many famous people. He is internationally recognised. He went to Arnold Schwarzeneggar's wedding and he's stayed with Jean Claude Van Damme. He has been involved with projects with Sir Jack Brabham, and he can rattle off a long list of well-known people, but it is like Pro just to remain at home.

'You know, Allan, they take me to all these flash places. They expect you to be in a suit and eat the most amazing meals and stay in big flash hotels. I'm just as happy and would rather stay home and have baked beans on toast.'

And when you get to know Pro that is just what he is like. Happy to potter about with his projects, to paint in his studio and wear his legendary shorts, thongs and paint-splattered T-shirts. In all the times I've since seen him, he has never worn anything else.

That is the *real* Pro Hart.

Postscript

We now await the auction of the Pro Hart ute in conjunction with Ford, RFDS and Pro. I look forward to completing the project. A lasting memory for me, of my time endeavouring to get this project off the ground and working with this great man, is the ute tailgate Pro painted. The auction is in October 2003 and at the time of writing (August) I'm touring the ute to art galleries around the country.

Reaping What They Sow

TOMMY, LORRAINE & SARAH McCORMACK

'WE HELP TO KEEP THE STUBBIE FACTORY
IN BUSINESS DURING HARVEST!'

'As honest as the day is long.' It's an old saying and one you don't hear as much in these dog-eat-dog days. But when I asked a couple of Tommy and Lorraine McCormack's customers what they thought of them, it was the response that told me something of the couple.

'Genuine, wonderful people, down-to-earth, very hospitable, give you the shirt off their back. Real bush Aussies.'

'Good, hardworking, honest country Aussies doing their thing,' was another comment said to me by one of their customers. I later met them for the first time when I went to their property, and what I had been told was soon confirmed. It was the first of many enjoyable meetings. Happy, bright and genuine comes across pretty quickly. A stubbie or a cuppa is always quick at hand.

'I've never had a trade or anything,' says Tommy. But what he lacks in trade papers he makes up in determination and hard yakka. 'We can expand the business still and that's the aim.'

Their reputation in the chaffcutting trade is so good as businesspeople that they do not have to advertise, and expanding the business will be necessary just to keep up with the supply and demand of their customers.

Tommy and Lorraine McCormack live on 40 acres at Parwan, Victoria. Both were born and bred in nearby Bacchus Marsh. Tommy didn't like school and left as soon as he could, when he was 14. Lorraine only ever had one job, and that was with the Taxation Department in the city, where she spent 16 years and rose to the level of supervisor. But like Tommy she is a bushie through and through.

'I first saw Tommy on a beautiful horse, and I wanted to meet him. We were both into horses when kids and we still are,' laughs Lorraine.

'I've done all sorts of jobs,' says Tommy, who is an outdoors man. No office for Tommy. He first worked in a plastic factory for twelve months. He then spent a lot of time in the market gardens around Bacchus Marsh.

'I even drove a sanitary truck part time years ago,' says Tommy with a laugh, and we swapped stories of the dunny-cart men who took away the human night-soil, long before the introduction of septic tanks and sewerage systems. Many people will remember those 'good old days'.

In my own country home town Charlie Dellar was the dunny-cart man, as us kids called it. As naughty young boys I remember with a mate lifting the trapdoor of an old dunny down the backyard of a house in town and throwing crackers inside to listen to the explosion echo in the confines of the dunny, hopefully whilst someone was seated inside. How we never burnt down a dunny is a wonder. But back to the McCormacks.

'I was driving a garbage truck at the time and agreed to help out take away night-soil for a couple of weeks,' says Tommy. 'I've worked all sorts of jobs. In 1971 I worked near Warburton on the Thompson River Dam scheme for twelve months. I was a dogman on cranes and then a rigger. I used to come home at weekends.

'Then I went back to the market gardens around Bacchus Marsh, until the Lerderderg River water diversion tunnel project started. I commenced shiftwork for two years, first working as a miner, then as a loco driver and finally doing drilling and blasting "on the face", as it was known.'

Tommy had grown up with a love of horses, something he inherited from his father Tom Snr. 'He always had horses, in fact he never ever got a driver's licence,' said Tommy. 'He always had a horse and spring cart, and later when we got a car my mother did the driving, he never had a licence, never wanted one. He had a bike.'

Tom Snr was a good horseman, a tall man over six feet. A Clydesdale horse team was a part of his job when he worked for Jim Madden, contract road-makers, and he used the horses with a large road plough to form up the roads. He also would break in the new horses each year. He later worked for the State Electricity Commission installing light poles and for twenty-seven years supplied coal for the furnaces at the local Bacchus Marsh Lifeguard Milk Factory.

He taught the horses how to work in unison in the large collars, towing logs. 'He was always a very hard worker, the old fella, a really nice man,' remembers Tommy.

That love of horses Tom no doubt passed on to his son Tommy, and it was that love of horses that led Tommy into becoming a registered horse trainer in 1973. Right through until 1994 he trained gallopers. 'Mainly in partnership with my brother John, with a line of gallopers we bred ourselves. I also continued with part-time work in the market gardens,' Tommy adds. (In 1978 his brother John was badly burnt in a local mill disaster and was unable to work and was back and forth to Royal Melbourne Hospital every day for nine months.)

Some people might remember placing a bet on one of Tommy and Lorraine's many horses. Bold Bronze, Kimberloch, Owen Moor, Squatter, Maldive Lad, Shooting, Right Show and Lady Bev were a few of their horses they rattled off when I asked.

'In 1982 we won enough money on one race quinella with Bold Bronze at 50 to 1 we came home and bought a ute, the one we still use,' says Tommy. 'It paid the highest quinella at the time and there was a write-up in the Melbourne *Sun* newspaper about it – $46,051 for the quinella.'

Tommy and Lorraine's horses were raced at country meets pretty close to home rather than interstate. Places like Woodend, Geelong, Avoca, Ballarat, Werribee, Kyneton, Bendigo and of course city races at Melbourne's famous Flemington, Moonee Valley and Caulfield racetracks.

'We never sold our horses and still have them in the paddock, we've got eighteen still. The oldest is Bold Bronze, now 30 years old.

'In 1986 I also started doing contract slashing for Werribee, Bacchus Marsh and Corio part time between October and January before the main fire season. I did it for seven years.'

Now, however, their business is their main interest. They love it. Tommy is 55 and Lorraine 50 but they work like younger people. Tommy still throws feed onto haystacks that take a long ladder to get to the top. He's not tall but strong and nuggetty, with a big-barrelled chest and strength that only an outdoor life gives a bloke.

'He gets a shoulder pain a bit now,' says Lorraine, but it's obvious that even at 55 Tommy still has plans of tossing some more hay around for a lot longer yet.

Another important member of the team is Sarah, their 18-year-old daughter, who has also grown up with a good work ethic. She was accepted by both Dookie and Longernong Agricultural Colleges, but is deferring for a year to help boost the family business, then goes to study at Longernong where she plans to specialise in soil and grain to become an agronomist.

This is a family of the land. It's in their make-up. It's life.

For Tommy, although he doesn't dwell on it, his hard work ethic and interest in chaffcutting might be owed to his grandfather. His grandfather, Eddie 'Darkie' Hehir, was born in 1901 and left school when he was thirteen-and-a-half. Darkie described his own early life in the book *Bacchus Marsh – An Anecdotal History* compiled by Geoffrey Camm (Hargreen Publishing Company, 1986). Darkie's life gives a clue to the methods and work ethic still evident in the current generations.

For a couple of months he worked chaffcutting for a cocky at Parwan for seven shillings a day, then moved to the big local chaffcutting mill, sewing bags. About 1400 bags a day came

through the machine, and the manager ominously had only one arm. Darkie had only a few seconds to sew up a bag of chaff – fourteen stitches across the top.

Darkie must have been a pretty good worker as he worked there for nearly three years. Sewing chaff bags is still carried on by old Darkie's grandson, by hand with a bag-needle and thread. 'He was always going to give me his own bag-needle,' says Tommy. 'He made it himself, but I never got it when he died.'

Darkie worked to bag feed which was used to feed army horses, then in the midst of World War I. His grandson still supplies feed for horses, but now it's for racehorses and pleasure horses.

But supplying feed to horses in the good old-fashioned way. 'We cut fresh oaten chaff and lucerne chaff every week. We also crush lupins, oats and barley in a grister, we do it the old way. Some people reckon we're mad but it suits us and I'll always do it this way.

'We will use other machinery as we expand, but I will always stook at least some of our harvest and manhandle it as we do, but we are also going to start doing round bales as well to help our expansion plans.'

'Tommy doesn't like change and he loves the old machinery and lifestyle,' says Lorraine.

But it is more than that. He also likes to supply top-quality feed for his customers' animals. 'I like to produce good quality feed, a standard of food I want to feed my own horses.'

Tommy enjoys working part time a few days a week at the local quarry doing maintenance, but loves to be back on his acreage doing what he loves best.

When they purchased their land nearly thirty years ago it was an open windswept place with not a tree on it. Today it is a lovely retreat surrounded by trees and garden and their love of the olden ways is evident by the amount of machinery, both useable and that which is simply now used as garden ornaments.

Their library is full of books and videos of old-fashioned Australian bush life, farming and such. The walls of their home are lined with photographic copies of old farming machinery, bush life, horses and animals. They may be seen to live in the past, but they really are working and living as they always have, with a strong commitment to the land.

All sorts of old machinery can be found on the place. They have five old Sunshine binders for instance, one being their main binder for the annual harvest. Some of the long list of implements include a Massey Ferguson combine planter, a Massey Ferguson 165 tractor, a 1926 Cliff & Bunting chaff five concave bladed cutter, a R. W. Hill single-bag three-knife chaffcutter, a Ronaldson tippet roller mill, a McCormack Deering grister, and a Cliff & Bunting knife sharpener. There's also two other Massey Ferguson tractors, other chaffcutters, binders, other mills, trailers, and much more. Many won't be restored but will be used for spare parts.

The Cliff & Bunting chaffcutter has been fully restored and is a much-loved workhorse. They bought it in 1997 from Syd Sloan, a farmer from Violet Town in Victoria's north-east. Even after they bought it, it stayed on the property for twelve months, before they finally trucked it home in September 1998. And another year went by while Frank Grech, a tool-maker from St Albans, restored it for them. By Christmas 1999 it was complete, and used for the harvest in January 2000.

The restoration was so good the McCormacks were a bit half-hearted about using it. 'It looked too good to use,' said Lorraine. Since then, however, it has been used and is now very much a part of working life on the farm. The double-bag chaff-cutter is now worth about $25,000 but they'd never part with it. Or their single-bag chaffcutter.

'Harvest time is a good time of the year here. We work until all hours of the night and then have a big meal in the shed at all hours. Tea is usually about 11 o'clock at night. There's always people around at harvest time,' says Lorraine.

Actually, I can vouch for that, in fact any time of the year is good at the McCormacks. Since meeting them, we've shared many good times in the shed, nicknamed the 'Parwan Pub', where their roast meals are legendary. Their barbecues are also legendary. The shed is legendary. If ever there was bush hospitality it is epitomised at the Parwan Pub. People love to come here, and always return, not only for the tucker, but the beer and the laughter. 'We help to keep the stubbie factory in business during harvest,' jokes Tommy with that huge infectious laugh.

These are rich people. Maybe not in the financial sense but rich in life.

So what is a year in the life of the McCormacks as chaff-cutters? By March each year they work and prepare their ground for planting. By May the 165 Massey Ferguson tractor and Sunshine 500 combine are in the paddocks sowing oats. By late October or early November, depending on weather, they 'make hay while the sun shines' as the old saying goes. But for them bringing in the hay is somewhat different to their neighbours who use big harvesters to either square bale or round bale. They use a Sunshine binder to cut and bind their hay into sheaves. They cut six runs of a paddock at a time, the binder cuts and carries six sheaves then drops them which leaves piles of 36 sheaves in one area of the paddock which they then stook by hand.

They build stooks facing north and south with a wind tunnel through the centre to help cure the sheaves. The sheaves are usually left in the paddock for about two weeks to cure. Then the carting in from the paddocks to the hay shed begins. Hard physical work. In about three weeks, Tommy, Lorraine and daughter Sarah will handle about 80 tons of sheaves. All in the midst of summer.

Tommy usually starts on his own very early in the morning, loading sheaves on his own into the back of his Holden one toner ute and onto a large tandem trailer. He works until lunchtime, but then the day is usually too hot. Work recommences late in the day and long into the night. Tommy always loads the sheaves himself as he has developed his very own style of loading. He loads from the ground and does not have someone pitch sheaves up to him on top as a stack grows.

'Many people can't believe I do it on my own that way. One old timer said to me one day he'd never seen anyone do it alone from standing on the ground, but it suits me and I got used to it. Yet, if I was up on top of a stack I can't load it as good. Guess it's just what you are used to,' he says matter-of-factly.

For many years Tommy and Lorraine supplied green feed to people who were showing horses at the Royal Melbourne Show each year. So popular was their feed that Tommy would make more than one trip down each day to satisfy clients. Now they have stopped doing it, but when people see them at the

Show they are still asked do they have any available feed.

Apart from their own 40 acres the McCormacks also grow feed on a 40 acre block owned by Tommy's brother, as well as another 20 acre block they lease from the local airport. Good friends Trevor and Barb Cairns own adjoining land and they also sell most of their feed through the McCormacks' business.

They all work in together, including son Ben Cairns, who is an apprentice at Longernong College who comes home at weekends to work on the tractor in the paddocks. The Cairns currently sow down about 400 acres each year, some on their own land, the rest on share-farming. Good friendship and a good working relationship ensures there's something for everyone.

Lorraine's brother Ronald and wife Joy are also available to assist, Ron being a qualified mechanic. They too enjoy the many barbecues in the shed at Parwan.

And although the business will grow as each harvest comes around, there's one thing that won't. 'Our lifestyle will never change, we'll always be doing what we do,' says Lorraine simply. Regardless of droughts or floods, heat or cold, the McCormacks love their lifestyle. And why wouldn't they, it's a great down-to-earth life.

Life on the land.

Life in a Treehouse

BOB PRUDHOE

'LIFE IS FOR DOING THINGS.'

Now 63, Bob Prudhoe has sailed over 2000km in a 65-foot wooden yacht through the inside passage in Alaska while fishing for sockeye salmon; he's slept in wilderness with grizzly bears; he's climbed Mount Kilimanjaro and to the base camp of Mt Everest; he's lived alone on an island; and climbed into a valley in Africa filled with crocodiles, baboons and deadly black mambo snakes. He's stayed with monks in monasteries in Tibet; he's worked on archaeological digs in the Guatemalan jungles; slept in the Kings Chamber of the Pyramid in Egypt – and he lives in a treehouse in the Yarra Valley Ranges.

And that is just scratching the surface of this man. He was a world leader in his field as a systems engineer, and invented many systems now used worldwide. He has lectured in many parts of the world. Now, though, his research is different.

Bob is researching his life and his place in the world, through art, and creating amazing things from nature is his life. He's been doing it for many years, but since retiring from the business world he is free to explore. And he explores life with a total passion. He has already lived the life of about three men. He is an amazing man. Eccentric – probably. Inspirational – definitely.

Born to Ernest, a coal miner from England, and Myrtle Constance of German ancestry, Bob's lineage goes way back and he's currently checking the relationship to the Duchess of Northumberland whose castle in England is called Alwich. The main tower of Alwich is named Prudhoe Tower. Bob is excited to learn that the Duchess is having a £12 million treehouse built, the largest in the world. Bob is going to see it and hopes to do some work on the treehouse. Alwich Castle is also the place where scenes for the movies *Rob Roy* and *Harry Potter and the Sorcerer's Stone* were filmed.

'My parents were quite tolerant of my curiosity – I was always curious and I get more so every day. I remember when I was about six I asked my mother, "Why am I living in my body?". She said small boys didn't ask questions like that.'

But Bob has spent a lifetime questioning, studying, learning.

'Now I am attempting to express myself with the ecosystem, the birds, the mountains, and the trees. Look at nature – it has awesomely interesting shapes.'

Bob's treehouse started life as the stationmaster's house, but when he took over it just grew and has never stopped growing. Not one nail has been put in any of the trees. 'I couldn't do that; I'd never put nails or bolts into it.'

For every piece of timber that Bob adds to his artwork, he

lights a stick of incense. 'To bless the timber and thank it for
its being.

'I've been seeking out the unknown god all my life, searching. My conclusion is: life is what you think it is, life is for
living. I don't like conventional. The best wisdom is to "Do
unto others as you'd want them to do unto you". To enter the
kingdom of God be a child: live with a willingness to challenge
convention. Convention isn't exciting. Be a master of manifes-
tation, not a master of limitations. Don't follow structural
religion, follow your own. Watch what we say, reap a good
harvest, think good thoughts with optimism, believe in tomorrow, look at the beauty of life, the flowers, nature, there's so
much magic. We manifest what's in our life, by lifestyle. Life's
a mystery, be a bit more tolerant, and there's got to be life after
death. I call it being in spirit.'

Bob's first trip was driving 26,000km through Britain and
Europe. He rattles off a few of the places he's been since then,
as I struggle to keep up with him: Tibet, Nepal, Indonesia,
Japan, New Zealand, North East and West Africa, Guyana,
Zambia, Burma, Thailand, Alaska, America, Canada, many
parts of South America, Guatemalan jungles, Germany,
Holland, Sweden, Norway, Finland, Greece, Turkey, Bulgaria,
Yugoslavia – he's even lived in the Seychelles Islands.

When he was a small boy, one of his schoolteachers at state
school told his mother that Bob was an idiot and that he should
be put to work, as he'd never achieve anything. His mother
ignored the teacher and later Bob, as a 16-year-old, went to
Collingwood Tech School, and later Footscray Tech studying
for a diploma in electrical engineering. He got a job with the
State Electricity Commission and worked at large power

stations like Hazelwood, Eildon Weir, Churchill, Rubicon and others.

He then won a scholarship to do a postgraduate diploma at Swinburne College in engineering, specialising in ventilation, air-conditioning, refrigeration and heating. The course started with thirty-five students, but after several years only two students remained to sit for the final exam. Fifteen minutes into the exam and one student gave up, as it was too hard. Only one student remained and passed the exam – Bob Prudhoe.

When he returned from an overseas trip he joined the PMG (Post Master General) and stayed for many years through to its changes to Telecom and Telstra and had long established his credibility in his field. He invented a world first – 'Fully automatic controlled environmental control systems for bulk potato storage'. He invented 'Phase-change material technology to protect critical heat emitting computers from overload'. He was also involved in other technical aspects like 'Defensive action strategy to protect critical computer areas from loss of cooling in times of failures of the normal system'. Such was the technical world in which Bob excelled and was a world leader. 'All good fun,' he says.

In 1989 he won a scholarship to do a Masters in engineering at RMIT, and was working on a PhD in alternative energy systems. He continued to lecture overseas, but in 1992 the Tibetan-style first home he'd built burnt down. The remains still stand and he hopes to rebuild it one day, but he moved across the road into and later bought the old stationmaster's house where he remains. With the land it sits on and his original home up the hill, Bob now owns about one-third of his whole street.

When the house burnt down Bob decided it was time to take off for a while, and ended up in a bar in Alaska. Bob made friends, and one man in particular later asked Bob if he would look after his house for six months while he spent time in mainstream America where he had business to attend to. In the time that followed Bob got stuck into the man's house and made it into a North American Indian version. It was on an island and Bob enjoyed his solitude there. He rebuilt and redecorated the house, without even telling his mate.

'Each morning I'd go down to the water and see what gifts had come in on the high tide – what the universe had brought me – and I put that driftwood and stuff into the house, sculpturing, building, knocking out walls, creating bay windows to watch the whales and the eagles.

'I had a small boat and I'd also go out to other remote islands and tow back wood to include in the house. Often I'd see many bald eagles, up to as many as thirty-four, soaring above me – it was magic. I'd also collect any of their feathers to add to a sculpture in the house.'

Once again Bob reinforced his secret – 'enjoy the journey'.

'Who wants to be a rigor mortis in a vitamiser?' is his blunt attitude towards death. His zest for life has made him many friends around the world. In Egypt, his friends are the Guardians of the Pyramids, who are custodians of significant artefacts and have shared special privileges, such as access to the pyramids – to meditate in the King's Chamber, to climb to the top of the pyramids at night and to participate in archaeological excavation of tombs. Bob has long held a love of archaeology and exploring ruins of ancient civilisations.

On a trip through Africa, Bob became the first white man invited onto a remote island, 200 miles from Mombassa. The people there are direct blood descendants of Prophet Mohammed. He was accepted into the tribe and was named Mustaffa Abdullah Zalim, which means 'Man of Peace'.

'The only problem was they wanted me to have four wives, so I got out of there. One wife would be bad enough. I had one for a year once in Indonesia.'

On another occasion, at the bottom of the highest waterfalls in South Africa (726 feet), Bob ventured into the dangerous valley, inhabited by crocodiles, black mambo snakes and wild baboons just so he could do some archaeological digging.

Bob always had an interest in mountaineering and bush-walking. 'I have always been fit,' he says. His first major walk was in 1965 when he was flown to Port Davey in Tasmania and walked back out through the rugged south-west wilderness.

In 1970 he climbed 21,000 feet to the base camp of Mt Everest – in a pair of shorts. Bob met world-famous mountaineer Sir Edmund Hillary as he was trekking to the base camp on Mt Everest. Bob didn't recognise him but commented that his backpack was a good one, a bloke called Hillary designed it for the first ascent of Everest. After Hillary had left, Bob was told, 'That was Hillary.' 'I admire him for what he's done for the mountain people, he's one of my heroes.'

Also in 1970 he climbed 19,340 feet to the top of Mt Kilimanjaro. He first started bushwalking at 24 and he says it's 'been a passion of my life'.

Danger seems to be a part of his touring. He spent time with the Dragon People on Komodo Island, because he liked their artwork. 'You have to be careful of the vipers, scorpions and dragons, though,' he says. 'Whenever I'd travel overseas to give a paper at one of the many international lecture tours, quite often I'd just take off afterwards and disappear and go off on some adventures somewhere.'

There is not enough space to write of all Bob's adventures here – this is but a few brief passages in his varied life. Bob is now looking forward to going to Hawaii to his friend's place to help build a similar place to the one he did in Alaska, and he's very keen to see Alwich Castle in England and work on the treehouse.

'Who wants to read letters when you can be sculpturing?' says Bob as he throws a bundle of unopened letters back onto the sideboard in one of his numerous lounge rooms. All rooms of his house are so cosy, so inviting, so interesting, it's hard to know what is where. It doesn't matter. All rooms are so enticing.

Timber plays a big part in Bob's life. I ask just what timber does he have here, and immediately he knows and rattles off a list as I scribble as fast as I can.

'Jackfruit, the beautiful carved Indonesian wood around the various doors. *Cupressus macrocarpa*, *Pinus radiata*, blackwood, yellow cedar, messmate, teak, redgum, ironbark, oregon, Norfolk Island pine, and some other woods from Guatemala.'

Somehow I don't think that was the entire list. But it'll do. It gives an idea of Bob's love of natural things.

Even the power pole outside his house was not safe from Bob's carving desires. 'When I heard they were going to replace the pole with a new one, I went and convinced the power company to allow me to carve a totem pole. So I did it in their work depot, then they installed it – the very first time it was allowed to be done, and it even made the newspapers. A pole enhancement project.

'Use everything – get excited – make something. I'm more excited than not,' he says. Look around his domain and you see he is certainly creative. He's 'exploring the arts' and has left the electronics world behind. Bob says matter-of-factly, 'What I did I did well. I was a world leader in that field, but now I'm into the art side of it all. A lot of people are still living in the dark ages, they need enlightenment, get rid of that which makes you feel heavy. By not loving yourself, you're afraid to do things. I've got enough in me to write a hundred books.'

Somehow I don't think he will – he's too busy at the moment living it all. Bob's work has not gone unnoticed. He is regarded as a local identity in his community, media attention of all sorts has come his way, including *Burke's Backyard*, *Location Location's Amazing Homes*, Channel 9 News, *Totally Wild*, *Postcards*, and a documentary for the College of the Arts. He has also featured in various newspapers and magazines including *The Age* and *Owner Builder* magazine as well as local papers.

'There's a great community here. I'm very lucky to be allowed to explore my art, not one inspector from the shire has troubled me over the years, and many have been here. It [his amazing home and sculptures] helps bring people to town. With the MMBW and the hospital gone it was dropping off, but now tourism is back, there's loving things happening in Warburton.' Yarra Ranges Shire Council spokesman James Martin says, 'Robert's house lends itself well to the council's idea of the artistic character of Warburton and it certainly adds vibrancy to the area'.

With all the building extensions, carvings, totem poles, etc. you'd expect to work in a great studio. When I arrived his tools were scattered by the roadway as he added more to his fence-line of art. His whole house and land is his studio workplace. He is almost oblivious to the cars that stop or slow down, people taking photos and quietly leaving.

'I use a power drill, jigsaw, router, angle grinder with sanding disc – and any other bits as I feel I need.'

Pick out just about any item in his house and there's a wonderful adventure story behind it that leads Bob into an excited state of memories of one of his adventures in some far-off place in the world.

It was when his mother, then 91, 'left her body' and became 'in spirit' that Bob contemplated his world. He was extremely close to her, and while thinking of her he expanded his home, and while it stands as a piece of art and is his 'research' he finds great contentment.

'Follow your spirit, lead an awesome life, follow your own creativity, challenge conventional thinking, go beyond the beyond to reach the unknown. Make possible what people think impossible. For me not creating would be like sitting at the bottom of a staircase and not going anywhere.'

Reading back through Bob's story I see I have made one constant error. I refer to his house. It is not a house – it is a home. A home built with much love and respect for all his environment, and for the people who share it with him, however briefly. I feel most privileged to have spent time with Bob and his amazing treehouse, and shall return to see it evolve more and hear more of his worldly adventures. I don't think he'll ever finish it – it somehow wouldn't be right, as it is a place of growth of all sorts. And Bob is at the helm of it all.

Postscript

I revisited Bob some months later to find him expanding his artistic work. He is now doing a fancy new sculptured fence.

Bob was also getting ready to travel yet again to the USA and Alaska. His good friends John and Belinda Maher, who built their own 65-foot wooden schooner called *Mycia*, are going to take Bob on another sailing trip through wilderness areas of Alaska's Inside Passage and down through British Colombia to Port Townsend in Washington State. They hope to be present at the annual migration of about 600 polar bears near Churchill, Hudson's Bay. Bob is also going to spend time with Peter and Marg Kormandy, heads of the local indigenous community, in a sweat lodge. He truly has many friends in many lands.

A final piece of wisdom from Bob? 'If you want to be a higher spirit, fly with eagles.'

Western Girl

DANNI SHOWERS

'OUT HERE, KILOMETRES MEAN NOTHING, IT JUST MEANS
YOU HAVE TO PACK MORE BEER.'

Danielle Showers ('haven't been called that since I was six'),
34, is a lady who is independent but relies on her mates.
She will have a go at anything but needs the company of her
many friends.

She works in the remote gold mines of Western Australia
and thinks nothing of travelling 1500km for a weekend party.
She has been the only female at times working in a hard and
rough industry at remote places, but most men regard her as
'one of the boys' and a mate.

I found her charming, casual and competent. She smiles
a lot. She didn't show it but I reckon there might be a temper
hidden away there and I'd hate to cross her. She totally loves
her dogs and horse and is a ute lover from way back. In fact,
she had emailed me after seeing my website on utes, and her

email letterhead said she was Senior Field Technician – Big Bell (Gold Operations).

My curiosity wanted to know what a senior field tech did in a remote gold mine. Numerous emails back and forth and I knew enough: 'That's it, I want to interview you, I'm coming to Western Australia.'

I don't think she really believed me, but I had made up my mind.

'How do you get from Perth to Big Bell?' I asked innocently, as most maps don't even show Big Bell.

This gold mine is so remote that, as with many other gold mining camps, all the staff fly in for two weeks' work and then fly home to Perth for a week.

Seven hundred kilometres north-east into nowhere? Hmmm, now let's plan this out. In Western Australia, 700km can take you into some pretty remote country. But over there no one seems to worry; 'You get pretty blasé to the number of kilometres,' Danni says. She drove a 3000km round trip just to go to a New Year's Eve party at Eucla.

I'd already met Danni in 1998. Only I didn't know it. With six utes and twelve blokes I drove Melbourne–Sydney–Perth and then to Corrigin to judge a ute show at the Dog 'n' Ute competition. We did it to raise money for the Flying Doctors. Amongst the huge crowd I'd asked Danni and her girlfriend, who both had dogs with them, if I could take a photo. And here two years later we meet again. It's a small world.

And so how do I get to Big Bell?

Big Bell Gold Operations helped us out. All I had to do was get to Perth. No problems. Waiting for me was another aeroplane to catch. The workers at Big Bell work twelve hour days from

6am to 6pm. Most of the seventy staff and 180 contractors fly in out of Perth. There's five planes a week to get everyone back and forth. As it's a company site, no one is usually allowed in unless there for a specific reason and all is approved beforehand.

There are usually 250 people working at Big Bell at one time. And so I eventually made my way to Perth by plane and then late the same day boarded a smaller aircraft and flew into Big Bell with about fifteen workers. The company would be assisting me to write a story about Danni and their business.

Danni was there to meet me. I threw my bag onto the back of the company landcruiser ute piled with bags of ore samples Danni had been collecting that day.

The company supplied me with my own accommodation, a self-contained unit in the workers camp. Excellent facilities, and all meals supplied, and beer at company prices. I was impressed.

Once I'd gone through the formalities and signed security clearance, I was free to have a shower and unpack. The next few days could be interesting to someone who had never been in such a place.

Big. Real big. Huge in fact. That's the best way to describe the mines of Western Australia. Harmony Gold, a south African company, owns Big Bell (Gold Operations). They have 1100 square kilometres of leases. Underground mines, mammoth open-cut pits and a huge processing mill are right near where I am staying in what can only be described as a purpose-built company town.

Twenty-three kilometres south-east is Cuddingwarra, a low-grade ore open pit; Golden Crown, Great Fingal is 30 kilometres south-east, working an old underground mine, and

new open pits. The Great Fingal has in the past given up 1.2 million ounces of gold.

Tuckabianna, south-east of Golden Crown and 50km from the mill at Big Bell, is an old open pit, now leading underground down a decline.

Big Bell is an old mine, open pits, leading into large underground operations. Three million ounces of gold has come out so far. And this is just one mine in one spot owned by one company. Western Australia certainly could be called one huge minefield. We in the east have no idea or appreciation of the worth this country has. Most of the company leases are owned by overseas companies as Australians are slow to invest in big operations.

Senior Exploration Geologist Brett Smith talks casually about the large figures of the area. They remove 100,000 tonnes of dirt and rock from underground a month, with a further 110,000 tonnes a month removed from the huge open pits. Normal mines chase gold-bearing ore in about a five-metre wide high-grade ore body. Big Bell operations averages 45 metres wide, and can be up to 60 metres wide, but it's low-grade ore compared to some other sites.

The equipment used is big too. One tyre on one of the trucks I'm looking at is worth $25,000 and only lasts about three months. In one scoop of dirt and rock the huge excavators pick up some 80 tonne.

I was really looking forward to the next couple of days, and after I settled into my onsite cabin, I joined the crew for a few beers and some tucker.

And where does Danni fit in to all this? Morning is often in the office on computer and then she heads bush in whatever direction the drilling crews are. 'They're out here somewhere,' she says as we bump our way on bush tracks in the Toyota Landcruiser trayback. Sure enough, a while later we spot them and cut across country off the track to where they are working.

Danni locates a series of small piles of dirt to work on. As the drill passes down through the earth, samples are taken and dumped. Danni has a pile of small bags and notes to take. She places some of the dirt in bags, tags them and logs them up in field notes. These are the bags that are sent back to Perth for analysis. Then it's back to the office to write up work on computer and send the samples.

Today, though, we go exploring and I meet many of the workers, geologists and drilling crews before an underground tour of one of the mines. Nearly two miles underground and I'm shown a tunnel that is now closed due to a rock slide, where a man died some time ago. This is sometimes an unstable environment, and I'm shown how they stabilise walls, and all the safety set-up. One tunnel is loaded with truckloads of dynamite and other explosives. Huge exhaust fans suck fumes out to the surface and fresh air is blown into the huge tunnels. These mines are unbelievably big. A truck passes us in the tunnel going to the surface fully loaded.

Underground is a whole new world, exciting, dangerous, claustrophobic, totally dark when the lights are off (I put my hand an inch in front of my face and couldn't see it), wet in places. A different world. Miners deserve big pay. Outside of the tunnel we are in a mammoth open-cut pit, with still another 600 metres to the top.

Danni explains a bit more of her life as we sit having a cuppa on the side of a bush track. It is hot and the flies are friendly,

but I'm having a ball. A few days here has really opened my eyes to another side of Australia.

'I work for the exploration department and get to drive around in the bush a lot. I provide field support for our drilling crews, drilling to find gold. Help the geologists and yell at the field techs!! (not really). Good crew and not a bad job all in all.

'I'm living in Cue at the moment, the nearest town to the site. Been there for nearly two years. The job is a fly-in fly-out of Perth but I can't stand the city so I choose to stay in Cue. Exploration work for us is usually one or two drill rigs drilling holes. The geos log the geology and I collect the dirt samples, which are then sent to the lab, on a truck to Perth.

'As senior fieldie it just means I also order any consumables and write and make sure everyone follows safe work procedures seeing as safety is so important in the mining industry these days. I do data entry on computer, geology logs, daily drilling reports and put assay results into Data. The afternoons I'm usually out in the field sampling off the drilling rigs. I am the Safety Rep, and write work procedures for Heath & Safety Occupation. Safety is a big thing here. I attend the safety meetings.

'Work gets very concerned when I go on my driving holidays because I have this habit of not quite making it back on time. They take bets on whether I'll be back on time. There is a whole board in the office dedicated to postcards. Most from me.'

Out here you meet some great people and Danni has many friends who keep an eye on her. Like Mick, who shows what friendship is all about. She broke down and he drove 900km out to where she was broken down and gave her his vehicle so she could continue on. They met up a few weeks later at the Tamworth Country Music Festival in New South Wales and on the way home, he drove an extra 600km to drop her off at work. He got her ute onto a truck and back home and then fixed the transfer case for her. 'Mick fixes everything.'

'I have my old dog Smudge to keep me company plus a new puppy. Also my horse in the backyard (it's now a one-horse town). I often travel down to Kalgoorlie on my week off. It's a bit over 600km away with 500 of that dirt. I usually don't see another car at all until at least 80km or less from Kal.

'I love my country music. Work suffers a signed picture of Kasey Chambers on the noticeboard. They are not quite so tolerant when I'm listening to Slim or Lee Kernaghan, though. I just came back from my third visit to the Tamworth Festival.'

I wanted to know more of the Danni Showers story and over the next few days running around with her while she worked I got to know her background. She confirmed she is a very independent lady who likes life, her friends, animals and travel. She gets out there and does it. And what of her background?

'I've been here going on three years, things are pretty relaxed, easy-going crews, seven on exploration staff; we normally work fairly close to the pits, although some exploration is a 100km away. From Cue to work and back each day for me is 40km, and then I travel around which could be another couple of hundred ks.

'Before Big Bell I was in Kalgoorlie for three years, between 1997 and 2000, lived pretty rough out the back of Kal behind the airport on the riding centre land. A friend, Fiona Brown, and I lived there with all manner of animals. She's studying in Kalgoorlie and also works as a barmaid She also loves dogs, horses and utes – and beer of course. She was going out with a friend of mine. Fiona and I have been mates for about six years now. We do everything together. We're a terrible pair. The riding school kids called us the ferals, which we thought was a bit harsh.

'Had a great few years around Kal, spent every weekend in summer on the search for water to swim in. Usually meant finding old pits out bush somewhere that had filled up with water. Bit salty some of them, but great to be able to swim. Initially didn't have a job when I arrived, but then for a month I was a "storeman", doing deliveries to the mines. Then I got into the Ora Banda mine, 50km north-west of Kal as an exploration fieldie continually doing sampling, then moved to the Mt Pleasant pit, and made senior exploration fieldie, to do computer GIS mapping work.

'Working from Kal was with big company, high pressure, huge exploration tenements, fifteen to twenty people in exploration work alone, numerous big open cuts. Ninety per cent of my work was 50km or more from the mine site.

'Prior to Kalgoorlie I was at the little mining town of Marvel Loch, south of Southern Cross. Again just me, the dog and the ute. My boyfriend had a job there. I worked as a barmaid at the pub for five weeks, then got a samplers job in the Nevoria pit. Geologist there taught me a lot. As I was paid by the hour, I chased a lot of hours. I learnt how to identify ore bodies, and the basics of geology and did ore spotting, and they also sent me to another pit nearby. I was the only girl at work and outside work. They were good boys, looked after me, guys pretty good I reckon. Only at Marvel Loch for a year or so but that was my introduction to the mining industry.

'Before that I worked for Springvale Station (Balmoral Pastoral Co) near Halls Creek, WA. Typical station work. 3am starts on mustering days. You have your own string of horses that you have to shoe – although the ringer I was going out with was much quicker at shoeing than me, so I got out of a few of them.

'He then became head stockman, so I had all the comments about the jillaroo's job being to keep the head stockman's swag warm. I hated being called a jillaroo, thought I should be a ringette or something! Great country, the Kimberley. Probably my most favourite job ever. I was a station hand bringing stock in to the yards. Did a lot of yard work – drafting, ear marking, de-balling calves. Initially I was the only girl in the Main Camp, but then two others arrived. I worked both the Main Camp and later the Station Camp. I worked the mustering season and when the wet season came I worked checking and starting the water pumps and fixed broken fences and all that sort of stuff.

'I worked in Queensland at Scartwater station before that. It was not far from Charters Towers, run by an eccentric old bloke, Charlie Heywood. He had all these mango trees and he would pick up all the old, rotting and green mangos that had dropped on the ground. These would then go into absolutely everything he made. This was usually a stew as I don't think his teeth were that good.

'He would employ young pilots at half ringer wage because they had a chance of getting flying hours with him. He had two light planes and two choppers. Shopping trips into Townsville were great. It was like I had my own personal pilot (well, I did for the trip at least).

'I worked with a blackfella called Herbie, and we went out on horses tracking mobs of cattle and brought them into the central camps, branded them and all that. It taught me a lot. We also got to go spotting cattle from the air in choppers. I was told I should go to a real station out west and that's how I bussed it to the Kimberleys.

'Originally I come from over east, at Porepunkah, Victoria. My parents owned a small property and a sawmill. I have a brother Alex, now 29, who's been doing fencing up at Derby, but is now studying engineering. Charlie, 27, is a young professional, he's with the Department of Agriculture in Beechworth, Vic. And I also have a sister Emily, 23, who is studying education and business at LaTrobe University in Wodonga.

'I went to school in Porepunkah and later Geelong Grammar where I passed HSC in 1986. Originally I did Ag. Science at university, and got a woolclasser's certificate, but never finished uni. I had glandular fever. I did get back to work initially on a horse stud, then in 1990 did one year at Glenormiston Ag. College, studying a horse management jillaroo course. Then I was able to get onto Thoroughbred Horse Stud and from mid-1992 to 1994 I worked as a yearling groom in the Hunter Valley, New South Wales. Prepared horses for the annual sales that we went to in Queensland.'

Danni is casual about most things, and seems to have adapted extremely well to the sometimes tough life of the bush. Her love of animals is very evident, and she talks of her mates as lifelong friends, even though many she doesn't see for ages. She has lots of bush mates scattered all over the country and they party hard when they get together. I really enjoyed our time together and know she will always be 'out there' somewhere. I hope we meet again.

My sincere thanks to Harmony, who operate Big Bell (Gold Operations) for flying me from Perth to the site, accommodating and feeding me, and supplying a vehicle and staff to give me access to their operations. Special thanks to Brett Smith, Senior Field Geologist, for his time and support, and to all the staff I met there who showed me around the various parts of operations. Next time, fellas, some free samples of gold bars would be nice!

Since we met, Danni has left Harmony. She is now in Kalgoorlie, still in the mining industry – this time looking for nickel rather than gold. Time for a change.

Bush Leather

SHARRON & GEORGE TAYLOR

'WE NEVER TELL ANYONE NO, WE ALWAYS SAY WE'LL HAVE A GO!'

They both grew up in Victoria's north-east, Sharron in the old gold town of Beechworth, and George on a farm at Myrtleford. They met on horseback while mustering cattle on the Bogong High Plains. George's heritage is the mountain country; his grandfather, Nick Clemems, was a Dargo High Plains cattleman, with a property at Harrietville.

Their daughter Erin had mentioned on my website one day her parents made leather whips and such, and I was instantly interested. Sure enough 'Lil Ez' was right and was not having me on – her mum and dad not only made all sorts of leather gear, but were damned good at it.

And so a few emails and phone calls later, I had confirmed a meeting and was soon on the road heading for the Victoria–NSW border country, just past Wangaratta. Australia was in the middle of one of the worst droughts on record and the country was dry. Very dry.

A few hours from home and I was following the rough directions how to find their farm. Dust billowed behind my ute like steam from an old puffing billy train on a busy day. God help anyone trying to follow me on the road; they'd be spitting dust for a week.

One more turn to the left and a few hundred yards along I notice the house as described. Lil Ez and her sister were at school, so it was her mother Sharron who came into the drive to meet me.

Once inside the back porch I meet George, her husband, who was busy plaiting a long stockwhip. We had cups of tea, cake and chit chat, getting to know one another. But as they had a business to run I encouraged them to continue working. I sat in the background asking questions and taking notes, while both got to work with leather in hand, Sharron making a long whip and George making belts.

My first impressions – damn true blue dinkum honest Aussies. There's nothing fancy or false about the Taylors; they are country born and bred, honest, hardworking – and a family.

It would be a longer interview than planned – we got on well and so it was morning tea, lunch and afternoon tea, and I was still there when the girls arrived home from school.

Their property north-west of Wangaratta, like many at the moment, has been suffering drought, and their stock is down. They lease 1000 acres and have about 150–200 Charolais shorthorn cross cattle. 'Always had cattle,' says George. Where he grew up near Myrtleford his family's farm was dairy and beef cattle.

Their business name SKT (pronounced Eskaytee) is made up from Sharron's initials. Though they make their goods using time-honoured, traditional methods, modern business practices are essential too. Sharron says their website http://skt.netc.net.au 'was a real boon when we did it. I built it myself with help from a niece, Amanda. The site opened it all up for us. It's our only retail outlet, it opened the world to us.

'My grandfather gave me my first horse when I was 14 and it just snowballed from there. I plaited a brow band for the horse's bridle and learnt more. I made all sorts of stuff for people and fixed their whips and horse gear, just repair work on horse gear for myself and friends,' she says.

'It became an extension from teaching myself from a book to other people showing me, and refinement from trial and error. I plaited my first whip in 1989 which I still have. Then I made another.'

Sharron laughs as she says, 'Anyway, I had an armful of leather gear, I went into a shop and said, "We make these, we live up the road, you need to sell these." He did, and still sells our products. Good quality and well made. Never the cheapest, but once they saw the quality . . .

'Actually my very first sale was a whip to a farmer, I can't remember how he got onto us. The first shop was a produce place in Wodonga; they bought a couple of whips and a set of horse reins,' says Sharron. 'Back in those days we had to scrimp and save until I could afford to buy the hides. Then when I got paid I'd go and buy more hides. No one told me about enterprise development loans or funding. We always did it all on our own. It's nice to know now we did it all on our own.

'In 1992 we did a trip to the Northern Territory. In the Todd Mall, Alice Springs, I wasn't expecting to sell much to a shop there,' says Sharron. 'But he kept saying, "I'll have six of them and twelve of them." I was flabbergasted. He's ordered and sold a lot of stuff, eighty belts at one stage, large seventeen-strand, top-of-the-range whips. That same bloke has now opened a shop in Beechworth and still buys from us.

'We've sold a heap of stuff through the saddle shop at Sovereign Hill complex in Ballarat. Whatever we made it's always been a steady increase, every time it was more. Whenever we'd go to stud cattle sales we'd take some gear and try and sell it somewhere along the way. We started the website five years ago.'

Make no mistake, this is a real business success – in the month prior to my visit they had exported their products to Scotland, Denmark, Turkey, Germany, America and all over Australia. They have also exported to countries like England, Canada, New Zealand, Poland, Japan. America is a regular destination for their handiwork, and more about some 'special' whips they make for America later.

They supply every state and territory of Australia, as well as well-known outlets like the Tenterfield Saddler and the Stockman's Hall of Fame in Queensland, Sovereign Hill in Victoria. They've come a long way since Sharron started plaiting when she was 15.

Sharron and George now make about 500 whips a year, in all sorts of lengths and types – bull whips, stockwhips, miniwhips, and of course those 'special' whips I will detail in full later. Promise. They also make about 1500 belts a year.

They are also kept busy making their other products such as

belts, watchbands, key rings, dog leads, hatbands, chinstraps, braces, knife pouches, watch pouches, wrist bangles, fly switches, auctioneer gavels, bridles, reins, stirrup leathers, hobble belts, breastplates, halters, cattle drafting canes and more. The order board on the wall was full of orders they were busy trying to complete.

'I always fixed my own whips on the farm,' says George. 'Sharron had been doing the business two or three years before I got involved – I was too busy on the farm. Sharron ("The Boss") taught me how to do it all. I mainly do the cowhide whips and belts which are hard on the hands when making them all the time. Sharron does the two-tone roo hide stuff mainly.'

So how did they meet, I asked? 'Twenty-two years ago I was on a four-day trip with a dozen others (including Sharron) on horseback, "salting cattle" on the Bogong High Plains,' says George. 'Sharron's cousin from Bright ran cattle on their mountain lease and I'd been helping them for quite a while. It was pretty country and that's how Sharron and I met – on horseback on top of the High Plains.'

People who work with horses know leather and it is a logical business for them as they know what people like and want in leatherwork. Quality is their number one priority in all their work, that's how they have built a good business reputation.

And where do they see their business heading? 'We are at the stage now where we have to make some decisions. We are at maximum capacity now with production and with increasing orders, we either have to employ people or look at changing direction,' says George. 'We are starting to address the situation now.' Obviously they have been discussing this and the future plan is still not finalised. 'The thing is, with hiring staff we have to train them to produce what we want and we're very fussy about quality,' says Sharron.

But both agree that the final future direction will most likely be less in volume and more specialised: highly valued items like trophy whips, collectors' whips and other much sought-after items.

The volume of work they can turn out is amazing. One order for Japan was 2000 leather arm bracelets, and just recently another Japanese order was for 3500. 'I worked it out I can make one every ten minutes,' says George. Daughter Erin is also adept at making them, and is often called in to assist after school hours. She also makes belts and has been a great help doing invoices and statements on the computer. Both Erin, 15, and little sister Sarah, 9, help their parents pack orders for shipping. It is a real close family business.

The girls arrived home from school while I was there, and 'Lil Ez' is no longer little, she's taller than her mum. When she first came onto my website she was always the youngest on site, just 10 then – she loved utes and wanted to have her say on site. She wants a WB Holden ute.

Of course, I had to see young Sarah's very own whip, and she gave a great demonstration on the back lawn on how to use it. Naturally when you live in a whip-making family you are good at cracking whips.

I was curious about a number of things related to their work. For instance, what sort of hides do they use? Greenhide is cured and salted cow hide. White hide is cattle hide treated with alum and salt, and red hide is cattle hide tanned with oil. Kangaroo hide is tanned using a vegetable tan and then grease. They buy their kangaroo skins from a dealer in Young,

New South Wales, who is also a plaiter. They mainly use Western Red roo hide, which he obtains only from special culling programs in conjunction with the NSW National Parks & Wildlife Service, involving all sorts of paperwork and special permits. Their business also has to have a special permit to export roo hide overseas. Being totally above board, they are very much controlled by government departments and other authorities like customs as to how their business operates.

I wanted to know more about the whips. 'Well,' says George, 'we make everything from a 3ft 6in kid's cowhide whip with plain cane handle to a 24-strand, two-tone kangaroo leather patterned handle "top-of-the-range" seven footer – and then everything else in between you can think of. We make custom whips for individuals, and bull whips for the USA with the plaited handle and whip incorporated into one. Stockwhips here usually have a cane handle with the thong separate.'

I asked about the dressing they use on the leather. Sharron said, 'We make our own special dressing, made mainly using mutton fat, paraffin, bees wax, lanolin and soap. The exact recipe is a bit of a secret. We developed it so that it suits our purpose.

'It conditions the leather, and helps the leather slip as you make the whip. When leather dries out it starts to break down. We give customers advice on how to maintain their whip if they need it.'

Of course I also wanted to know who were the sort of people who buy the whips and gear. Why would someone in America buy an Australian-made whip?

'All sorts of people buy them, not just farmers or people who work cattle. Enthusiasts,' says Sharron. 'We sell to a lot of local whip-cracking clubs, a lot of people are just collectors, hobbyists. One of our customers in Scotland works for a circus as a juggler. We also supplied to an aerialist with Circus Oz. She bought a pair of special silver bull whips.' Sharron brought out a piece of leather that had what looked like silver foil on top of the leather. They also make metallic whips. The combination of the special foil-type look, just like gold leaf, added to leather makes the whips a very special product indeed. 'She wanted one to shine and reflect off the lights as part of her circus act. So we made it for her.'

George also mentions some of the people they have sold to over the years and it's obvious they have a great clientele worldwide now. Word of mouth has been good for their business.

'Another of our customers is a woman who conducts trail rides in Canada. Another is a performer at a big hotel in Turkey. Nine out of ten of our customers are enthusiasts. One man in Georgia USA owns a radio station, and he is a keen antique gun collector. He also has an extensive whip collection, and he's bought a few whips off us.'

Dunlop Australia got them to make a heap of fly switches and small miniature whips from the business to give away as presents to Japanese who were visiting the company in Australia. The mini-whips crack just like a full-size whip.

Sharron has even made a saddle for a wooden rocking horse!

They supplied cat-o'-nine-tails whips for a convict re-enactment. It was the cat-o'-nine-tails that also attracted a new customer who was after 'special' whips. It is those whips that daughter Erin doesn't like to promote so much. She even rubs the name off the order board in case someone should see it.

Sharron looked at George and said, 'Should we tell him the other part of the business?'

'Yeah, why not,' says George. 'Erin will be mortified we've told you.'

They are quick to add that it's not their main business.

Between them they informed me a part of the business comprises special whips. 'We supply whips to America to a couple of people who are dealers in whips for people who have bondage websites and businesses in the sex industry. One was so keen on our product, he wanted us to make nothing else but stuff for him and he wanted all the American rights and he'd sell them all over the country for us. But it wasn't us – we supply him some, but we're not into that sort of stuff.'

We had a laugh about it all and I said they'd probably make more money supplying that and they could test the products out in the bedroom. They laughed and we joked a bit, but it is a sign of the honesty of the people that they have knocked back the offer and continue to look after all their other customers as well.

The man in America still gets some, in fact there was an order on the board at the time. We knew we'd have some fun with Erin when she came home, and of course as soon as she did I told her that her parents are going to give her a WB ute as soon as they sell some more sex aids to America. Erin blushed and laughed, and said no way. She too saw the funny side of it all.

Sharron adds, 'Erin is now doing camp drafting events with her horse and we want to spend more time on that, so we'll probably sell some products at events.' It is obvious they are looking at new directions with the business. 'Long term, say in ten years at the most, we will only be making special whips, collectors' items,' she says.

Recently they read where a man was going to ride a horse from Darwin to Corryong to raise money for cancer research. Sharron contacted him and told her she'd donate a special collectors' whip to raffle off. The raffle raised $2500 but the winner re-donated it back and then it was auctioned off. The whip they donated to Campfires Against Cancer was auctioned and brought $2550.

It was in a special presentation wood and glass box made by Sharron's father. It was signed on a calico backing by country singers Lee and Tania Kernaghan, Adam Brand, Troy Cassar-Daley, Melinda Schneider, Sara Storer, John Williamson, Felicity, Paul Kelly, Tamara Stewart, Brendan Walmsley, Korey Livvy, Travis Sinclair, Adam Harvey, Garth Porter and others. The Taylors also gave an armful of the little whips and all the artists signed on the night of the concert which was held in Albury in April 2003. A great family effort and a wonderful gesture by the whip-maker family from the bush.

It was time at last for me to hit the dusty road once again, so we swapped some Uteman gear for some SKT gear, signed some books and took some photos and said our goodbyes. I felt I'd made some new friends and I'd return.

I now wear SKT belts and in my ute is a great stockwhip which I crack to announce my arrival each time I go to various friends' farms.

From a do-it-yourself hobby to a tiny part-time enterprise,

the Taylors have shown that enterprise, dedication, persever-
ance and skill can develop into a full-time business and be
taken to the world.

A great Aussie bush family and great bush leather.

Yeehaa, where's my horse!

The Paddleboat Man

KEVIN HUTCHINSON, OAM
'KEVIN REALLY IS A LIVING TREASURE.'

The throb of old large engines, white hissing steam, the thrashing of paddles that swish through the water. Steam whistle carrying a distinctive call through the air. Sounds of another era. Freedom of river life.

Nostalgic paddleboats.

Memories of the days from about the late 1850s to the early 1900s when the paddleboats were king, on the large inland rivers of the Murray and the Darling. A time when towns relied on the huge boats to carry all sorts of goods up and down the rivers. The riverboats were the workhorses of the time, transporting just about anything from people to wool-bales to any supplies to a distant property or camp. They were the lifelines of all the settlements on the riverbanks, delivering anything, including the mail, to tiny remote settlements.

In Echuca in 1872, on the Murray bordering Victoria and New South Wales, some 240 boats loaded or unloaded at the port. It boasted Australia's longest inland port, 1.2km long. In 1880, Echuca handled about $5 million in wool and other supplies.

By the 1920s, it was all pretty well superseded by faster, more modern transport. Many thought the riverboat days were dying and would soon be well and truly dead.

Today, however, the Port of Echuca is still home port for the world's largest collection of paddle-steamers and an authentic working paddleboat steam port, with a thriving paddleboat trade based on tourism – and weddings, restaurants and a host of other activities.

I've spent a lot of time in Echuca over the years. In fact, I try and stay in the same room at Steampacket Inn, built in 1876, each visit, a room that overlooks the wharf and where I can write and look out the window that is right in the heart of the action. Soaking in the atmosphere of the place – great for a writer.

Every day you can hear the steam whistle of any number of paddleboats as they arrive or depart from the wharf, you can see the faces of the people on the decks of the boats as they take in a cruise on the ever-changing waters of the mighty Murray. In recent years the Port of Echuca has come into its own and its future looks bright.

I came to Echuca to find a man. I wanted to find someone who was living and working on the river, a person who had a strong connection with the Murray. I knew I'd find him, I just didn't know who he was.

When I told the Manager of the Port of Echuca and local

Tourism & Community Development Manager, Frank Ryan, why I was in town, he said immediately, 'We've got just the man for you.'

And he was right. Kevin Hutchinson, OAM. I'm sure no one will mind if I nickname him 'The Paddleboat Man' – he deserves it.

Kevin was with a young group of men on the Port of Echuca getting ready for a day's work when Frank and I walked up. After introductions we went down the riverbank and onto a floating workshop amongst the paddleboats. Nearly three hours later I left to meet up with Frank for lunch. We conducted the interview, we had a cuppa tea and I took a heap of photos before shaking hands and leaving him to his work. Kevin even put me into a small dinghy and we put putted our way up and down the river so I could get some photos from the water.

'One of my sons is the sixth generation in my family to work with timber. My Dad was working as a carpenter and joiner on the Williamstown dock, but we moved to Mildura in 1945–46 for a drier climate due to the ill-health of one of my sisters. I was about 5 or 6 when Dad and Mum loaded up the old Chev and trailer, my sisters and brother – Janet, Shirley and even loaded up the chooks and we went to Mildura. Dad was then a self-employed carpenter and joiner. Phillip our other brother was born in 1955.

'As a kid in Mildura I sometimes went with Dad to the redgum sawmills by the river and saw the paddleboats. I was always interested in them, and then I got a bike and would always go down to the river. The 1950s was when the riverboats were probably at their lowest ebb. There was the

Rothbury, the *Gem* and *Avoca* there and about half a dozen others tied up – never to go again. I basically watched them cutting up the *Gem*'s engines to get the brass and copper for scrap metal. There was asbestos everywhere.

'Opposite the Mildura wharf on the New South Wales side they scrapped a lot of boats. There were only five people left working in the area then. Anderson's sawmills still did boat repairs and Norm and Bill Collins, who were second-generation riverboat men ended up teaching me a lot. I used to just go there at weekends and watch and learn. They taught me how to select, cut and carve timber, as well as things like steam bending and caulking and doing boiler repairs. I watched them, from 1958 to 1974, a long time just to learn out of interest and later I was paid. It was there I gained a lot of knowledge and confidence.

'In 1958 I started my apprenticeship in carpentry and joinery with J.N. & F.G. Perry in Mildura, but at weekends I'd always go down to the river and the paddleboats – watching the decline. With my apprenticeship I was helping to build houses, motels and learning all facets of the building trade which I did for 16 years and four months.'

Kevin knows a great deal about the history and the work on boats like the *Wanera*, the *Rothbury*, the *Pevensey*, the *Ranger* and more in the sixties and seventies, enough to fill a whole book.

In 1973 the paddleboat *Pevensey* was in Mildura but bought by the City of Echuca. Kevin took time off work and came to Echuca as a deckhand and then, as he says, 'threw my hat into the ring' and took the job on council wages to help rebuild her. For the first twelve months he worked on all the buildings in the port, the Bridge Hotel, the wharf, the bond store and then started on the *Pevensey*. (Originally built in 1911 of timber and steel, 111 feet 5 inches long, 23 foot beam, weight 136 ton, 20hp twin high-pressure steam engine, and carries 100 people.)

'I was in charge of the rebuilding and we had up to six people working on it. We had to reframe the whole boat, bending angle iron, which isn't easy. We spent three years working on it – cut every single plank and nothing was finished unless I was involved. It was a difficult task but I knew I could do it and we had a good team. I've always found if you "pull something apart and put it back the same way it stood the test of time". I've always been quite wary of using new products.'

Pevensey was completed in 1979; Kevin said that timber quality nowadays is a problem as the best redgum is 200–300 years old and harder to get. They had all the best timber locally cut from six sawmills.

'It was the very best timber. It cost about $1000 a foot to rebuild the *Pevensey*.' It came out of the water on 4 March 1975 and went back in on 28 October 1976, but we then lost eight months on the project due to the river flooding.'

At the time the council was short of funds, so in January 1976 Kevin started work breaking up footpaths and other council jobs until they found money. He was away on holidays when they rang him and said come back as they now had funds. He then worked on it with his team to finish it in 1979.

'In September 1979 I was laying brick paving in the streets when I was told to go see the engineer. He said, "We want you to fix up the *Adelaide*." So I had another boat to work on.'

The *Adelaide* at the time was high and dry and sitting in the

park opposite the Bridge Hotel. Originally built at Echuca in 1866, she weighs 58 ton, is 76 feet long, with a beam of 17 foot, twin 36hp engines and carries 12 passengers. She is the world's oldest wooden-hulled paddle-steamer still operating.

'And so on 5 June 1980 I went back to work on boat-building, with $150,000 to rebuild it. We had to jack it up three feet, reframing and replacing all the timbers. But then we had a four months interruption – working on the filming of the TV miniseries *All the Rivers Run*. So during the filming I worked as engineer on the *Pevensey* (renamed the *Philadelphia* in the TV show) from October 1982 to March 1983. I was seconded by the council to the producers, Crawford Productions, to look after the council's interest. It was really a good experience; they were friendly people and always 10-hour days from any time. We might have started at 2am till whenever, whatever the filming schedule.'

All the Rivers Run won national and international acclaim and all these years later Echuca still receives many overseas visitors who simply want to see where the miniseries was made. It has helped Echuca cement its reputation as the river-boat capital of the world.

'Years later I was on a boat and all covered in soot and grime and the star of the miniseries, Sigrid Thornton, was visiting and came on board. She was dressed up but just threw her arms around me, not worrying about her clothes.' (Port of Echuca Manager Frank Ryan told me he saw Sigrid at a function not long ago and she said to make sure he said hello to Kevin. And since then Kevin has caught up with her at the reunion of the TV production held in late 2002.)

'On 4 March 1984 the *Adelaide* was put back on the water.

Finally in October 1985 she was recommissioned by Prince Charles and Lady Di.'

Kevin went back to general maintenance work on the wharf and other areas of the port until 1986 when the *Enterprise* (owned by the National Museum in Canberra) arrived on the back of a truck in Echuca. Kevin and his team had another boat to work on for restoration and by October 1988 it was fully restored and on Lake Burley Griffin in Canberra.

Whilst working on it another project came their way. In 1987 a nearby council had bought a barge from South Australia and planned to make it into a paddle-steamer; however, the project was shelved, so Echuca bought it and between 1987 and 1990 Kevin and crew had another project – but it was put on hold until the *Enterprise* was finished.

'The very same day the barge went back into the water in 1990, the *Alexander Arbuthnot* arrived from Shepparton for restoration.'

She was built in 1923, the last steamer built on the Murray during the riverboat trade, but ended up lying idle until she sank at her mooring in 1947, until raised by a group of Shepparton volunteers in 1972. She's 76 feet long, with a beam of 15 feet 3 inches, weighs 46 ton, has a 10hp engine and carries forty-seven passengers.

'It had to be rebuilt from the stem to stern,' says Kevin. 'Eventually refloated after two years, and then recommissioned some eighteen months later in December 1994. Been running in service every day since. I then went back to normal duties around the port again.'

I took a ride on the *Alexander Arbuthnot* later in the day cruising the Murray at a leisurely pace, and yarning with the crew. It gives you a chance to go back in time, to dream of other days and, especially if you are an author, to 'feel' the lifestyle. My parents were on holidays at the caravan park at the time so I gave them some tickets to enjoy the ride the very next day. When I visited Echuca again in November 2002 the *Alexander Arbuthnot* was undergoing more restoration work.

By now Echuca – and Kevin's reputation – was widespread when it came to paddleboats. Kevin was asked to go to Renmark in South Australia to give some advice about another paddleboat, the *Industry*.

Later he heard that businesspeople Gary and Irene Byford had bought the *Hero,* the only problem being it lay at the bottom of the Murray River at Boundary Bend. Since 1989 Gary had been determined to revive the boat. The river beat him and he also had back problems, but he was determined, even though the boat with the sides burnt off it had sunk to the bottom of the river and was full of mud.

'In January 1998 he decided that this was it,' says Kevin. 'He loaded up all his trailer and gear and went there and in mid-February 1998 he finally got it up, from being submerged in mud – when I saw it I thought it's a very ambitious project. But Gary is a very resourceful man. If Plan A doesn't work then you move on to Plan B. The whole of the Byford family have a keen interest in the restoration of the *Hero*. It's a real family affair.'

Kevin showed me some photos of the *Hero* when it first rose to the surface from the murky depths of the Murray. Most people would not have thought it possible to resurrect the boat, but Gary was going to put his money where his mouth was and the expertise of Kevin Hutchinson would see it through and do it.

'The *Hero* arrived in Echuca on the back of a truck in February 1998 and it went into our yard onto bearers and we started work on her. We've made new angle iron frame ribs, completed new stem planks, all new decking, all new upper works, and new steel engine beds. Gary wants it as authentic as possible, so there's absolutely no welding on this boat; it had to all be done with riveting.'

Now sitting in the water at the dock at Echuca is that boat where this interview was conducted. Kevin and his crew now have their own new floating workshop barge. For years Kevin just used to cart his tools up and down the riverbank and work on the banks in all sorts of weather. The barge is right next to the *Hero*. At the time of writing it isn't finished but by the time this book is being read it should be. When I later returned to Echuca the *Hero* and the work barge have moved into the wharf area extension and Kevin was still working on the boat; however, since my last visit the huge new boiler has been installed. No welding – all riveted, and painted in dark green and gold. It looks magnificent. Kevin now hopes the *Hero* will be complete within twelve months.

As owner of the *Hero*, Gary Byford is enthusiastic about Kevin's work. 'For us to build this boat has been a big task,' he says. 'Much bigger than we originally thought. Knowing what I know now, it was probably too ambitious a project when we started it. Our business wasn't as good then as it is now. However, having Kevin work on it is great. I am pretty particular; I like things right, with attention to detail. I have three blokes working full time in our premises doing all sorts of things like riveting, etc.

'But as the shipwright doing all the timberwork Kevin has

been excellent. He just knows – because he knows. He is one of the "old school" and been taught by the "old school". We've looked at all sorts of people, even naval architects, and the boats go in the water and don't work as well as the ones built a hundred years ago. A hundred years later and we still rely on people like Kevin. He just eyes something off and knows how it's to be done.'

To wander around the *Hero* and see its rebirth compliments of Kevin and crew, you see the real tradesmanship of a man totally dedicated. A dedication he's passed on to those who have come to work with him.

Kevin Hutchinson has been working on the river since 1966. Thirty-six years of work. 'This is only the second job I've had since leaving school,' he says. 'Basically they gave me a hobby for a job. I owe much to my wife Ruth, who has stuck by it all through the years. We celebrated our thirty-six years of marriage yesterday,' he says with pride. 'It was a big thing for her to leave everything to come here and she's put up with my working all hours, being away, running late and more for many years.'

'Even today Kevin still comes down to the wharves as late as nine o'clock at night just to check everything is locked up and "his" boats are okay,' says port manager Frank. 'These boats are his life, he lives and breathes them. We are very lucky to have him.'

So here's a bloke who has spent some 36 years working with timber around boats. Almost a lifetime of knowledge and experience. But I wanted to know more, and find out what Echuca will do when Kevin finally retires – what have they done to ensure that Kevin's knowledge is not lost. There were still some unanswered questions in my mind. So I wanted to delve into Kevin's background and more.

There was much more about boats Kevin was telling me, and his recollection for dates and putting everything in chronological order was amazing. But I cannot devote more space to all the knowledge he has about all the boats on the Murray. We'll have to save all that for another book. Hopefully Kevin will write it all out one day if he ever gets to sit and reflect.

'Well, in 1979 I got my Engineer's ticket. You have to do a two-hour oral examination and four two-hour written examinations. In 1985 I also got my Skipper's ticket, which meant you had to have 1000 hours of driving experience on boats. So I used to do that on weekends to get the hours up. You have to do practical exams in lighting, navigation, maths – calculating fuel and all that sort of stuff.

'So I can now work on them from the very bottom to the top. I can build them, maintain them and drive them,' he says with a laugh. Over the years Kevin has gone on to train ten skippers and ten engineers. He's also overseen three apprentices in boatbuilding, which is a five-year trade course. They spent time doing theory at Footscray Tech and then hands-on working on boats under Kevin's direction. 'Andrew Cook has left us and gone on to his own business fixing boats in Mildura.'

Others are still working with Kevin. Andrew Neilson has finished his time, and still works at the post. One local man, John, who came to work on a Jobskills program for a month, ended up going right through and even worked as a volunteer for six months, then got onto a further course and eventually sat for an Engineer's ticket. He has been working as an engineer on the *Alexander Arbuthnot*.

'Tom, a volunteer, is a retired motor mechanic and a very good one too,' says Kevin. 'And Adam Auditori came to us for work experience at the age of 13; he went on to top his class in his apprenticeship and is now a shipwright and also a paddleboat skipper. His wife, Eleanor, is a tour guide for the Port of Echuca.' (I met her, as she was about to take a tour later on. She too is very enthusiastic. It's a real family affair around here.) Since my last visit Adam has now started to work in his own business on boats along the Murray.

As we were talking, the steam whistle of the paddleboat *Canberra* blew as it steam-paddled by. 'There goes my son now,' says Kevin matter-of-factly. 'What do you mean?' I asked.

'My son Neil is the skipper on it today. He's also a qualified steam engineer. He works on it and other days on the *Emmylou* or *Pride of the Murray*. He's worked for the Port of Echuca for about five or six years. He's 29 and is married to Kerry. Our other son David is a cabinetmaker and joiner. He lives in Melbourne with wife Tracey and son Jacob.

'You've got to have the backing of a good work team, you need good bosses to make it work, you need the backing of everyone, especially the wife.

'We have all taken something (paddleboats) that had no future and given it a future and I get a real buzz out of seeing them being enjoyed by people.'

I had written about nine pages of notes, when I finally said to Kevin, 'I've written all this and you still haven't even mentioned you were awarded the Order of Australia Medal.'

'Oh, I wasn't going to brag about that,' he replied.

Frank Ryan had previously shown me the citation hanging

half hidden on the wall in the office, otherwise I doubt if I'd ever have learnt about it from Kevin. I had to push for more details.

'It was for Community Service in the restoration of paddle-steamers or reads something like that,' he says. 'I must say, I was very proud when they asked me if I'd accept it. Governor Davis McCaughey presented it to me in April 1990. I rang my sister in Melbourne and said you'd better have a look at page eight of the paper, you might know someone, but I didn't tell her what for. She rang back all excited and then before long I was getting phone calls from all over Victoria as people read it. I still haven't found out who it was that recommended me for it.'

I think that typifies the sort of man Kevin Hutchinson is. A dedicated worker, really an unsung hero and one who has made an enormous contribution not only to his community but also for Australia.

Kevin is pretty up-beat about the future of the paddleboats. 'It'll all keep going now. We've trained the young blokes to maintain them. We've got the people to drive them. And people want to see them. Now we just have to consolidate what we've got.'

The work of Kevin, his team and those community-minded people around him have brought considerable prosperity to Echuca. The television miniseries certainly helped and Kevin says he especially sees it in the 'fresh lot of foreign tourists every time – you know they are re-enacting it all in their minds as they walk around the place'.

What they don't know is the man in the overalls and old towelling hat just quietly going about his daily work has had an enormous amount of input into what is there today. Without him it may all have never been restored.

In Echuca it is 'full steam ahead' literally, in more ways than one. Port manager Frank also talked to me later of the future. 'We've got a steam heritage festival now. We have a twenty-year reunion of *All the Rivers Run* coming up later in the year. There's the opening of the new steam train line and the expansion of various projects such as the rearranging and upgrading of the cargo shed, restoration of the *Ada* and *B22* barges and the consolidation of everything we have. We have a steam traction engine for restoration, as well as other equipment.

'As our current slogan says, "There's nothing else like it in the world". It's authentic. The whole theme here is authenticity and Kevin personifies that at all times. It's all heritage here and it has to be correctly handled. Kevin likes to tinker with an old mini Casey engine that was used to inspect the railway line years ago. Guess who will be using it to do regular maintenance checks on the new spur line?'

But the final word on paddleboats should be Kevin's. 'I think paddleboats are the greatest; they all have their own ways about them. They have got a bit of a soul about them.'

'Whistle'

SYD WILSON

'I'M A BIT SCRATCHY ON MY EDUCATION BUT
HARD WORK NEVER HURT ME. I COULD BUY A NEW CAR TOMORROW
FOR CASH – IT JUST WOULDN'T BE A BLOODY MERCEDES.'

Imagine it if you can. I am in a country kitchen in Penola, South Australia. I am being held in a Japanese short arm bar by a 90-year-old man and I am unable to move. He applies a bit of pressure and looks me in the eye. 'Now I could break your arm very easily,' he says. I believe him. We laughed.

We sat down again and I reached for the glass of port and lemonade. 'Dad has one every lunchtime,' says his daughter Heather. If that's his secret, who am I to disagree.

Syd 'Whistle' Wilson put the defensive arm hold on me that he learnt many years ago when he was a 'special constable' during the war, to stop brawls in a timber camp he was working at. It also helped him tackle and subdue a killer.

Syd Wilson is a remarkable man.

They bred them tough in the Wilson family. Syd, known as

'Whistle', now 90 years young, is one of seventeen children of the late Fred and Annie Wilson. He is the eldest and all except three of his siblings are still alive. Syd is a tall man with a straight back and a very firm handshake. Deafness hasn't stopped the man's involvement in all that goes on around him or his sense of humour.

His still lives in the home he built 66 years ago with timber he cut himself from the forests. He stills grows enough in his large garden to keep the local old folks home well supplied with fruit and vegetables. He still carts redgum posts to cut into firewood. He still helps out as a wool-classer in shearing sheds. As a keen shooter and hunter all his life, he says he's now just the 'gate opener' for his younger shooting mates. He was still shooting feral animals in his eighties up until 'the government took guns away from shooters after the Port Arthur massacre'.

Two years ago he found out he had prostate cancer. 'Some days I'm not worth a cracker, but when I reached 90 I felt quite satisfied.' He still goes out in his tin fishing boat. He still drives his four-wheel drive ute.

Yes, Syd Wilson is a remarkable man, still working since he left school to become a blade shearer. 'I'm a bit scratchy on my education but hard work never hurt me, I had a go at anything and everything.'

Leaving school at just 12 years of age, Syd had limited education, but was willing to work. 'My Dad had a large team of workhorses and I helped on a property crutching and started as a rouseabout in shearing sheds for Fred Kidman, who taught me how to shear sheep with blade shears. He was great, old bloke,' reflects Syd. 'I also worked in a few sawmills and then would go shearing in the season. We worked in the sheds from 7.30am until 5.30pm.' By the age of 16 Syd was working as a faller, an axeman felling trees for a sawmill with another good axeman, Harry Brown from Tasmania. 'We were felling trees and making redgum sleepers. We used both axes and cross cut saws – and pulled logs up onto skids by hand. Later they brought in horses to help. We did a lot for sleeper cutting. Later I got my own mill and it took a couple of years to get it going.

'One day I was asked to take the T-Model Ford to the Penola railway station and pick up a girl there. She was a Scottish woman called Grace, with a Scottish twang in her voice and was a nice singer.'

Syd ended up marrying Grace in 1937 and they had three daughters, Heather, Barbara (deceased) and Nancye.

'I was still working in the forests in 1939 when I wanted to enlist in the army, but the director of Woods & Forests in Adelaide said "Back to the Nangwarry sawmill, Wilson". As I was a faller, we weren't allowed in the army. I was listed as being in protected employment, and required to stay there until after the end of the war. I also worked in the timber camp and many of the workers were religious blokes dodging the army by working in a protected job. The Nangwarry Timber Mill were making ammunition cases and parachute cases for the war effort.

'I became foreman, then later mill supervisor. I was recommended by the mill manager and made a "special constable" attached to the police to help look after the prisoner of war camp, which held Baulks and Italians at the 14 Mile Camp, near Penola.

'Fights broke out every night in the timber camp and it was my job to break them up. Also at night I used to go fox shooting. I was pretty fit and always went to a gymnasium, and learnt to box. As a special constable extra money was paid to me via Wood & Forests. Grace was always terrified when I'd get a call to break up fights and waited by the gate for me.'

It was as special constable that Syd became involved in an incident which even today seems to bring back vivid memories. 'Paddy O'Leary was a nice fella, a commando type, big, strong and a very good worker, but when he was drunk he'd just go mad and was a handful for me. I'd had a couple of brushes with him before. "Shorty" Ballard was a stacker of cases at the mill, O'Leary belted Shorty up once before when they worked together on the roads, and O'Leary had been sacked. Anyway, I was called out to attend and here was Shorty, he'd been in a tin bath and was covered in petrol. O'Leary tried to burn him, but he finished him off by stabbing him in the neck.'

When Syd had entered the men's living quarters at Nangwarry mill, with rifle in hand, what he saw would stay in his mind forever. Shorty was barely alive, and O'Leary drunk and aggressive. 'When I knelt down and asked who had hit him he replied "Paddy". We took Paddy to the mill office and the Mt Gambier police came and collected. I was sorry to see him go because he was a likeable fellow. I could see both sides of him – tall, smart, well liked, but every weekend on the grog.

'The doctors at the court hearing said Shorty wouldn't have been able to talk because of the wound, but he did and that's the way it was. O'Leary killed Shorty. He used to wear leg gaiters like those worn in the army. We later found them covered in blood, but washed, hidden behind the tin bath. I had to accept it, but I didn't like to see him hanged.'

It was obvious that this incident made an impact on Syd. Paddy O'Leary became the last man hanged in South Australia.

After the war, on 1200 acres all timbered with stringybark, with his father and three brothers, Syd set out to supply timber. They were contracted to supply 300,000 fence droppers to the Lands Department for the soldier settlers.

Syd was in his own mill for about a dozen years but when another man went bankrupt, it broke Syd's business as well. He had been supplying 3x2 inch fencing and 6x4 inch redgum posts.

'So for the next six or seven years I worked as a farmhand,' he says wistfully. 'Too long, I was going nowhere.'

Timber was always part of Syd's life and so were trucks. From South Australia over the years he's carried 25 ton loads of small logs to Victoria to Yallourn power station, Ballarat, Geelong, Mildura, Albury and to various parts of South Australia, including Adelaide. His trucks over the years included a 7-ton Diamond T, a GMX 6x6 and International.

Syd reckons he was the first person to use a chainsaw in Australia. It was made in Finland and brought to Australia by a Canadian who was looking to expand into new territory. 'I was asked to go into the forest for an afternoon for a demonstration and I bought one plus one for another bloke, the only two in Australia at the time.'

Syd was only in debt once. 'I've never had much money, but if I didn't have cash, I didn't buy it. I could buy a new car tomorrow for cash, it just wouldn't be a bloody Mercedes.'

Not only did Syd and I spend time at the kitchen table, but he took me into his garden and to his sheds. He gave me a cross-cut saw to add to the collection, and one of his old rabbit traps. I always like to have something of the people I interview and have bought or been given all sorts of crazy stuff over the years.

I asked Syd how he got the name 'Whistle'. He laughed when he said, 'Back in the thirties and forties I was a keen bike rider, and entered race competitions. I'd be in the middle of the pack somewhere and when I wanted to get through towards the front, I'd whistle out and my mates would let me through and away I'd go. The name sort of stuck.'

Without a doubt the lifelong interest for Syd has been hunting and shooting. A bedspread is made from kangaroo skins, another is a floor rug, a wall has deer head trophies. 'I used to load all my own shot,' he says as he shows me his loading equipment. A huge photo on the fridge is one of Syd on a horse with his hunting dogs.

Daughter Heather sums up Syd 'Whistle' Wilson. 'He's a good man, a hardworking man. He's mellowed over the years. We love him. He's just an amazing man.'

The time has come when I must leave Syd and hit the road. It has been an interesting afternoon, but I have some miles to do to get further along the track. He sees me to the ute. We shake hands and once again I am impressed by the man's firm handshake.

His daughter was right in what she said.

That he is, truly an amazing man. I won't forget you, Syd.

Banjo Maker

LAURIE HARVEY

'MUSIC IS A GOOD SUBSTITUTE FOR ALCOHOL AND DRUGS
AND NO ONE EVER DIED FROM TOO MUCH MUSIC.'

'If you come over the mountains look for a Ramrod Creek sign but if you take the highway the other way then go past a couple of 60km/h signs and then a couple of 80km/h signs and at the first 100km/h sign there's a road on the left called Little Dick Range Road. It's a yellow place and there's . . . well, there's a different vehicle in the driveway nearly every day. It's a quite nice little place in the bush.'

It was a typical bushie attitude to instructions on how to get to a point. It probably would have been easier if he knew exactly how many kilometres from town to his house, but bushies use landmarks of all sorts to describe how to get to a place in the bush. When I got off the phone I realised I still didn't know if he was a couple of kilometres out of town or 50 kilometres up a mountain highway. Didn't matter, I'd find it. That was all I needed.

I've had far worse directions in the past on how to get to a place. Once I had to meet a bloke whose name I didn't know at a farm I didn't know except a general district, and whose brother lived nearby but I didn't know his name either. All I knew was the sort of ute he owned. And I found him, by asking a farmer who scratched his head and worked out roughly who it might be and possibly where he might live.

I knew I had to meet this bloke, the banjo maker. I had cut out a newspaper clipping. I kept it as I knew one day I would interview Laurie Harvey. I rang him nearly 12 months later and we had a yak. I then rocked up to his home. A copy of his sales sticker says it all: *The Rechabite handmade, old time, mountain banjos. Made in the mountains of far-east Gippsland using indigenous timbers and traditional Aussie ingenuity.*

A banjo maker who is a flower grower living in the mountains with a bunch of utes and old motorbikes. Yep, just the sort of bloke I like to interview.

Since our meeting, Laurie tells me, he has a beautiful lady in his life: Michelle, who is a descendant of the Monaroo people of the Guri nation. 'A true princess with the looks to match', as he puts it.

Laurie has many friends, both male and female. His three children include Andrew, 22, Gabrielle, 15 and Tom, 4.

On the surface you may look at Laurie Harvey and not see beyond the dreadlock hairdo of this big man. However, I had time to spend with him and learn more of this man's life. He admits to having had a wild side to his earlier life. 'Music is a good substitute for alcohol and drugs and no one ever died from too much music. My ambition is to become a 100-year-old banjo player,' says Laurie.

Motorbikes have played a large part in the life of Laurie Harvey. His first bike, when he was 19 years old, was a 500 Triumph. 'Old Pommie motorbikes were cheap and they always came with heaps of spare parts. So I ended up with a shed full of spare parts over the years.'

Laurie has had nine Triumphs, thirteen or fourteen BSAs, maybe more, three Royal Enfields, two Kawasakis and 'more Hondas than I can remember', he says. His 1979 Harley-Davidson shovelhead chopper was finally sold to help him gather a deposit on the house he now lives in.

Over the years he has belonged to motorbike clubs including the 'Brain Donors'. 'We use only use 10 per cent of our brains and so we thought we'd donate the rest to science.' He also belonged to the 'Warburton Highway Destroyers'.

'All my life I wanted bikes, my mother didn't want me to have one and I wouldn't want my kids now to get involved in motorbikes. Funny how age changes your attitude.'

Laurie still owns a number of bikes including two 1939 BSA 600s, a 1947 BSA 500, a 1954 BSA 350 and a 1952 BSA 250. He has many parts for the same brand scattered around his one hectare property. 'I've always mucked around with engines, the first effort was at 12, when I built a go-kart with a lawnmower engine.'

His other vehicles are his one-tonner 1957 International ute, a 1954 15 hundredweight traytop, a 1964 three tonne International and 'another half-dozen others scattered around people's properties awaiting me to collect them. I find them in paddocks everywhere.'

And what does Laurie drive daily? 'Whatever is going at the time and that fluctuates daily dramatically,' he says.

Laurie described himself as just a normal knockabout, who 'values friends more than money'.

Laurence John Harvey was born in Worcestershire, United Kingdom and came to Australia with his parents in 1969. Now 42 years of age he says, 'My family were the original 10 bob pommies. We migrated here to live in the Upper Yarra Valley, near Melbourne. I left school to start an apprenticeship as fitter and turner. However, I didn't like working in a factory.'

He left and went to the western district to learn shearing and then worked in South Australia and New South Wales. 'I became the fastest rouseabout for Grascos, picking up for eight men who were all top shearers. Shearers taught me all about unionism, socialism and the Australian lifestyle.

'I then worked in sawmills in the mountains of the Upper Yarra Valley and then I would cruise up and down New South Wales to Queensland six months at a time in various sawmills.

'Later I was three years as the maintenance man on a pig farm. Then at the age of 30, I took on an apprenticeship for flower growing, a four-year course, but I didn't finish it, as I was qualified to be a nurseryman and they were paying good money. I then ran a nursery before working a few more sawmills.

'For three or four years now I've grown my own Australian native flowers. I particularly like working in harmony with the environment growing banksias, waratahs, etc. and still experimenting with potting mix made up of old sawdust and sand.'

As well as his hectare with house Laurie has another hectare of rainforest further east.

'Working in sawmills I saw the total injustice when they would sack people for no reason. Once, nine people were replaced by one saw bench and their attitude was they couldn't care about those people that no longer have a job. All the logs were sent to Japan.

'My parents had been president of the Conservation Society in Yarra Valley. Since I was a teenager I have had great appreciation for the natural environment. Growing up in England we experienced what it's like when we don't look after the environment. We were there when the Thames was disgusting, before they cleaned it up. We came to Australia to see it following suit, only twenty years behind in ruining the environment.

'I became a shop steward at both sawmills and on a pig farm. My grandfather was a shop steward in the UK. The most irritating aspect of the logging industry is the perpetual ignorance of the rich to inflict on the rest. When the RFA (Regional Forestry Act) came in I saw the need to become active. We are paying a contractor to supply another country with our forests, when in their own countries they have given up years ago.

'I started by writing letters to newspapers expressing my viewpoint. With the election coming some months ago, I got involved in the politics and we organised protests at catchment areas on the Snowy River.

'The future must be that we take control of our own resources. We need to make more independent furniture factories, that we have no clear felling, only sustainable selective forestry, employment in the towns, primarily small factories and associated businesses such as flower farms. Australians are intelligent and creative and we're capable of using our resources and should not be told by multinationals.'

Laurie is a passionate conservationist, but it was time to

hear more of his banjos. 'My banjos are a classic example of Australian ingenuity, making do with what we've got. The clamps on them come from old motorbike spokes, cut down and rethreaded. The fifth peg comes from a ferrule petrol line of a Stromberg carburettor off a Holden to tension the fifth string of the banjo.

'All the brassware is cut out and carved from scrap brass. From red ironbark I made the bridge and glued it onto huon pine. People reckon you can't glue red ironbark. Well, I soaked it in acetone and wiped all the oil from it and repeated the process until it no longer turns pink. It's then you can glue it.

'The banjos are made from mountain ash fiddleback scraps left over from sawmills and usually about four inches by four inches and up to nearly two metres long, that would simply be thrown into the wood chipper. Instead, I collected them, took them home and recycled them as banjos. I love timbers. Now it's hard to get good blackwood fiddleback timber, though. Most of the high-quality timber in East Gippsland is now gone – never to grow back again.'

The sound of rain on Laurie's tin roof mixed with those from his homemade banjo fill the kitchen with a raw twang that I love. I've always liked bluegrass music and particularly the banjo and harmonica. The old saying 'it was music to my ears' rang true, and we shared some time over a cuppa or two, and he showed me his various instruments: banjos, guitars, and even a homemade bass made from an old tea chest.

I didn't know how Laurie would react but I knew I had to own his special banjo. I wasn't going to wait for him to make one, I had to own *that* banjo. To my surprise he agreed to sell it, and his only comment was he'd have to get to it and make another one quick smart as he plays in music groups around the district. Can I play a banjo? No. Will I ever play a banjo? Probably not. But who cares, it is now a proud addition to my life and sits by my bedside. I just like to look at it and feel it. It's special. Different.

And fretless. 'I don't make banjos with frets,' Laurie explains. 'The very first ones made by the hillbillies in America were fretless, it was not until much later that they made them with frets.'

What I liked about Laurie's banjos is that they are hand-made and each is individual. He has a great passion for the timber and he uses fiddleback.

'Mountain ash fiddleback is my favourite. It is a term used to describe the wavy pattern in the grain of some trees, and I just thought it would look good for making the body and neck of a banjo. Some banjos vibrate in the neck and you adjust the volume by having clothes pegs on the end of the tuning peg heads. However, the banjos I make have a 12mm square stain-less steel rod which goes right up the middle of the neck and makes the neck unbreakable. I also fill the neck with blackwood so it is not hollow. I make the neck as dead as possible so that the sound stays down at the skin area of the instrument.'

Laurie is a tall and barrel-chested bloke and reckons one of the reasons why he took on banjos was because he was too ham-fisted for the guitar, but the banjo suits him fine. And he has his own thoughts on the timber, particularly how fiddle-back occurs.

'Common theory is fiddleback only occurs in old trees and that the weight of the tree makes the grain bend. Well, I have seen fiddleback in young trees and I reckon it is the result of trees grown on windy hills. I think it would be real worthwhile if they put blackwood plantations on windy hills. Just imagine the number of fiddleback musical instruments you could make if you had whole plantations of the stuff. Of course, those plantations would be owned and operated by the people of East Gippsland.'

And why is fiddleback so good to make instruments from, I wondered? 'Fiddleback is so dense a timber that it's like butter or like hard cheese to carve. You don't have strips of grain coming out,' he says. 'It's beautiful to carve and work with.'

Although he spent a year planning his first banjo it didn't take Laurie long to hasten the projects. 'After that first one, the second took me two months to make, then the next one only two weeks to create. The neck on the latest one only took two hours to carve.'

And what do people think of his creations? Renowned American bluegrass musician and banjo picker Reed Martin gave Laurie's banjo the thumbs up. 'He thought it was really cool,' says Laurie. 'He tried one of the banjos at Harrietville, near Bright when we were both playing there at a bluegrass convention.

'I like most sorts of music but I don't like blues. I like lively and happy music. I listen to opera and am a member of the Gilbert & Sullivan Society, like my parents. Been in it for four years – it's a good way to meet the girls. My parents are very much into it and so it's a good way to spend some time with them. I was a sailor in *HMS Pinafore*, and also was in *Pirates of Penzance*.

'When I was a teenager I was into guitar and songwriting. Now I'm in various bands. I play the bass in an Irish pub band called *Tinkers Cuss*, and I play the fiddle at festivals in a blue-grass band called the *Flatlanders*. I also just started my own band, called *Murrungowar String Band*, in which I play the banjo and we play at old halls and such.

'I believe in this self-sufficient living in the mountains style and if you play music in the country your social life can even become annoying because there is so much socialising. It's so related to the hillbillies. I like the music of the Appalachian Mountains of America, the Australian bush songs, folk music, even Cajun music from the deep USA south. The music is not complicated.

'I made my first banjo seven years ago purely because of lack of money, but I did import some parts from the USA and I spent too much money. My completed banjos, individually handmade with unusual timbers and parts I'll build to customer requirements and it will just take me about two weeks to make.

'This summer I want to commence building a stone miners cottage with a two-storey attic on the rainforest block I own further east from here – I want to add a rocking chair for the verandah with no fences and let the wild animals feel they can take refuge in the gully. There's heaps of lyrebirds in the forest there, and maybe I can get them to sing along. It's a beautiful spot. The cottage will also have cypress pine, which is termite proof. It's about a thirty-minute drive from Cape Conran on one of Victoria's best beaches.

And what of his flower growing days? Laurie loves to grow flowers and hopes to create a market for his plants in a few years' time. 'I just love to live in harmony with the environment,' he says.

A flower growing, banjo playing, opera loving environ-mentalist. It's a long way away from the heady days as a member of the Brain Donors Motorbike Club.

The rain still drizzles down as I prepare to leave him to his quiet patch in the bush. It's time to hit the road. Packed care-fully behind the seat of my ute is a parcel. A special mountain made one-off mountain ash banjo by Laurie Harvey – the banjo maker.

The Moving Man

JOE BOWEN

'I CAN REMEMBER BEING IN MUD AND SLUSH UP PAST
THE TOP OF MY GUMBOOTS.'

It's November 2002 and by the end of next month Joe Bowen
will move house for the last time. He's been doing it for over
fifty years and moved about 3000 houses. Other people's houses
of course. Joe's only moved himself a couple of times, from
Avoca to Maryborough, Victoria. The house he still lives in
with wife Beryl he moved onto the block in 1956 and he's been
there ever since.

Joe Bowen, 70, is a third-generation house mover. In the
early 1900s, and right through the 1920s, both his grandfathers
George Walkley and David Bowen from Avoca moved houses
with wood-fired steam traction engines.

Joe has great admiration for the old timers who worked
so hard, his family included. 'Jesus, they done it hard, we
don't know what work is. I always worked hard, but nothing

compared to the old fellas. I don't know how they lived so hard. No ice, no cold drinks, they lived on bully beef, terrible heat or cold, no fly repellent, always bogged in sand or mud up to their knees, miles from anywhere. Later they carried an old IXL cast iron stove to cook.

'The large floats built to carry the houses and towed by the trucks were first timber ones before steel. My grandfathers and Dad's floats in the 1930s were built from old wooden poppet legs that they got from one of the old gold mines. The frames were about 35 feet long, and had four wheels on a fixed axle 13 foot wide across the back. They used it right through and into the late 1940s, but it was later replaced by steel-frame floats in the early 1950s that were 38 feet long.'

His father Fred grew up working for a tinsmith in Avoca and his uncle for a blacksmith down the road, and they'd meet for lunch each day to discuss daily life. Later his father went share-farming in the Mallee district before joining Avoca Transport, and moved to Maryborough in 1944 when Joe was only 12. Avoca Transport also had an Atlantic Fuel Agency in Maryborough. Mr and Mrs Bowen were working to make a good living for their family. Joe had five brothers and two sisters.

'We were pretty tough, I guess. Even on Sundays we'd go out to a relation's farm and we'd take our ferrets to get some rabbits, and Dad would find an old tree and we'd help cut it down with an axe, and then split the timber up with a hammer and wedge. Always working. Dad was battling for his family. They did it tough in those days.'

At the same school as Joe was a young girl called Beryl. Her parents had moved from Cheltenham in Melbourne to take over a bakery in the town. The two youngsters later joined the same youth club. Beryl would become Joe's wife in 1955.

'As a kid of about 13 I used to go away working with Dad moving houses when school holidays were on. I started in 1945 as the billy-boy making the tea for Dad and the gang,' he said. 'I remember the first job I went on. It was to move a house from a farm and we moved it eight mile into Avoca. We had an old Reo Speedwagon truck to move it.'

By the time Joe had finished fourth year at the local tech school, he'd decided to join the Victorian Railways at Newport in Melbourne to complete a five-year apprenticeship as a boilermaker. He also completed National Service in 1952 in the engineers. At the completion of his apprenticeship he was straight back to Maryborough. 'I couldn't get back to the bush quick enough,' he says. 'Dad was moving houses for G.L. Ross and so in July 1954 I joined Dad to work moving houses.

'In those days the roads were bad. Many areas only had rough dirt roads, with deep corrugations, so deep you could lie down in them and you'd hardly be seen, they were so deep. And sand. Always got bogged in sand.

'Dad and the gang would take a house from Maryborough and transport it right up to say Mildura, much of the road not sealed from Ouyen to Mildura, and it'd take two days. You'd work all week then catch the train home late Friday and arrive in the early hours of Saturday morning. You have a haircut Saturday morning, mend your leather boots, and leave on the Sunday night train back to Mildura. We moved houses all over the place.

'We moved the first area school way out to Murrayville in the sunset country. We moved many railway homes to Mildura. Places like Pyramid Hill, Manangatang, Woomelang,

Cohuna, Wycheproof, Rochester, Tallangatta, Heathcote, Bendigo, Laanecoorie, Warracknabeal, Horsham, Litchfield, various parts of Gippsland, and as far away as Robe in South Australia, out the back of Broken Hill in New South Wales.

'You wouldn't believe it – once we even took one from Talbot to Nathalia district then one from Nathalia to Talbot within two miles of the first one. The Talbot man moved to Canberra and the other owner from Canberra moved to Talbot.

'Often it wouldn't be from Maryborough but houses moved from say old farms into townships. We moved some from Pyramid Hill to Rochester, Pyramid Hill to Bendigo, and off farms and into nearby towns like Horsham, Warracknabeal and many other places. There's nothing you can't move, even brick veneers.'

Joe still has two large floats with eight tyres across the back, the 38 foot long frames made from 8x4 inch RSJ steel licensed to carry 55lb per foot.

'The best load ever carried was 50 ton but don't tell Vic Roads that. Rules were bent a couple of times,' he laughs. 'Often they'd be over 10 ton just in tiles on the roof of some houses. The widest load we carried was 43 feet from spout to spout and the longest was 70 feet in one load, although some of the army huts during the war, I believe, were 80 feet long. Nowadays, though, with all the regulations you wouldn't be able to do half of what we did in the old days.'

In 1950 the Housing Commission began to make prefabricated homes in Maryborough and shifting them all over the state. Phelan Homes had a contract to build and move 1000 homes. Over the years they built some 4000 homes. After about 600 homes were built they started to take private orders as well. Work was plentiful.

'They were churning out nine new homes a fortnight, and we had to move them out otherwise production would stop. We'd sometimes move two houses a day into Ballarat, other times it'd be two a week to various parts of the country. Between 1952 and 1959 we'd do 30,000 miles a year easy, which in those days on those roads was a lot. When they enlarged the Hume Weir we moved about twelve homes to Tallangatta for the State Rivers & Water Supply Commission.

'In the early days we moved houses up to 20 mile a day, or 10 mile a day if they were in one piece. It'd take four or five days to do most jobs. Many times we had to remove roofs and verandahs and then reinstall them. We never touched trade jobs like plumbing, plastering, electrical or brickwork, but the lifting, moving and relocating and setting up again, we did it all.

'In 1951 G.L. Ross bought a new truck. It was magnificent – an International L190. The twenty-seventh in Australia. Eventually we bought it and I've still got it, fully restored and we still use it.'

Joe and I walked up to his huge sheds nearby and he backed the truck out into the sunshine. 'Now that is a truck,' he says with pride. 'I've got three more of them on a mate's farm, but this one we rebuilt the motor a few years ago and did it up. Not too many trucks on the road still earning their keep after fifty years, mate. She's done well over a million miles and she's a real truck,' he repeats.

'You know when we first got her, we'd park her around the back and cover her with a tarp; she was regarded as such a top truck, we didn't want everyone to know we had her. I know a bloke who when they first came out even offered to drive one for nothing, no pay, just so he could drive one.'

Joe has great pride in this truck and many, many memories of being 'on the road' with her to many places.

'In 1956 the whole of Victoria was wet with floods. Bloody terrible. I can remember being in mud and slush up past the top of my gumboots, trucks bogged and working in all sorts of weather. Gees it was hard.

'In 1959 I starting driving a truck to and from Melbourne for a couple of years, and then went interstate truck driving, carrying mainly posts and cement to and from Adelaide. In between I'd also help move houses. Then one day I got in Dad's ear and said "Why don't we do this for ourselves?", so in 1962 we decided to become house movers on our own. G.L. Ross was then more interested in farming; he sold a lot of his gear to Phelan's, so we started on our own, Dad, brother 'Toby' (Dennis) and myself. We started F. Bowen & Sons on 1 April 1963. We bought the International L190 truck off Ross, the one I still have.

'Our first job was moving workingman's quarters and houses for a bloke; one to Broadford, two to Wallan and four to Port Addis near Anglesea. Then we had trouble getting our money from him. I went from £35 a week to £20 a week as a result,' says Joe. 'It'd bring a tear to a glass eye,' he says with a laugh.

'Anyway, we got more work, brother Peter joined us in 1965 and brother Max joined us in the late sixties and we had another bloke outside the family as well. We also leased the Shell Service station in town which Toby and Ian ran and we'd help.

'Then in 1974 we got the carting contract to take flour from the mill for Granny Davis Bread. We carried three loads of flour in three bulk tankers to Melbourne every day and also two trucks of bagged flour. While some worked on that others still did house moving. At one stage it was twenty-six times to and from Melbourne every week with 22 ton a load. We did that right through until the mill was sold in 1980, the year Dad died. He was still working until he was 72, and died when he was 80.'

By now I was onto my fourth cuppa tea which Beryl kindly kept coming, along with biscuits, cakes and even lollies in their nice and neat home in Maryborough. The day was wearing on, but Joe is not short of a word or two and we don't worry about time. Beryl is off hunting for some old photos of some of the houses they've moved around the state. Joe is enjoying sharing his memories.

'We did have one accident on a big job near Wilcannia, New South Wales, in 1977. We had a lot of work to do on Vidale station moving a shearing shed, cottage, sleeping quarters, mess hut, meat store, shower block, woolclassers hut and contractors hut. All to be moved to higher ground as the owner was sick of being flooded out. The shearing shed alone was 110 feet long and 36 feet wide.

'Anyway, we had chains hooked up and when we called out if everyone was ready one bloke who had his hands on the chains said yes, and when we took off the chain tightened and took off part of his finger. The accident happened at 8.20am and by 10.10am he had been collected by Royal Flying Doctors airplane, flown to Broken Hill and was all stitched up and in hospital. I can really relate to just how good the Flying Doctors are.'

Joe's sense of bush humour often comes out in conversation; for instance he was relating how he was thrown out of the Ivanhoe pub many years ago for not wearing a shirt. 'Because

I had my shirt off I was asked to leave the pub. I couldn't believe it, especially as it was a stinking hot January day and the blokes with blue singlets on were hot, filthy dirty and sweaty, but they were allowed to drink. I walked across the road to the shop. I said to the girl behind the counter "Have you got any dry biscuits?" Yes, she replied. "Well, give them a drink then," I said. She didn't see the joke.'

Time rolls on but Joe has many yarns about moving houses, and it's time for another cuppa tea anyway.

'You know when they were building the Tullamarine Freeway in Melbourne, I reckon we must have moved about 40 homes that were in the way of construction and moved them to various parts of the state. One ended up in Red Cliffs, near Mildura, others to Gippsland, Swan Hill, Queenscliff, Ballarat, Manangatang, Castlemaine, Harcourt. Even twelve of them came into Maryborough. There's six homes in our own street we moved here.

'Between 1954 and the end of 2002 we moved about 3000 homes all told. We never ever had a major accident in all those years. As well as homes we moved shearing sheds, barns, all sorts of stuff – even shops. I remember near Great Western we moved three large silos – standing up – across paddocks for about eight miles. The farm had been split up amongst the family and we moved the silos from one to another. They were 22 feet high to the cone at the top which was another 6 feet high. They were also 22 feet across. Quite a sight seeing them moving across hilly paddocks. I've got it on movie film, as we have a lot of the moves.

'It was always amazing how the jobs grew in size. They'd ring you up and say we have something one size to move, but when we turned up it was often much bigger than originally stated. We got on well with Vic Roads over the years and never had any real hassles with them. We were honest and kept on the good side of them, except for a couple of times. I remember one young bloke wouldn't issue a permit and I said, "I been moving houses since before you were born, don't tell me my job." I received a fine only once for not having a current permit: it was in the mail, but a smart copper wouldn't believe me and it cost me $18. I said to the cop, "What are you doing here, I thought you'd be at the wedding." "What wedding?" he replied. "Your mother and father's," I replied with a laugh. He didn't see the funny side of it.'

Joe's business saw many repeat customers. One family near Maryborough used his services to shift fifteen to twenty houses and sheds on and off their property over the years.

And so next month comes the last job. Moving a shearing shed from one part of a property to another at a farm near St Arnaud. It will bring to an end a long family tradition.

And what did Beryl think of Joe being away from home so much all those years? 'I didn't worry about it, I just knew he was out there doing his job, now I look back and wonder how I ever put up with it, but we survived.' She would have been well occupied all those years Joe was on the road providing for the family. Their children are now all grown. At 45, Dean's work and sculptures grace many collections, both public and private.

Trevor, 39, is a Melbourne fireman specialising in rescue work, and is married with three children. Their daughter Deirdre, 34, is married with three of her own children and is a clerk with McPherson's Printing Group in Maryborough.

I had to ask Joe what was the hardest job he ever did. 'Well, it was a double-storey joint, but the bottom floor was shot to buggery so we just took the top floor off and moved it to the new block where it was turned into a granny flat.'

So what will life be for a Moving Man once the business is sold and it's all behind him?

'Well, I don't mind a bit of fishing, mate, have been doing it for many years along the Darling. And me and Beryl will do a bit of travelling around. I've never been up the centre through Alice Springs and that, so we'll certainly get around. Me back's gone ratty, she's finished, so at last I've learnt to say no, and now it's only one job to go and I'll be packing it in by Christmas.'

You wouldn't expect a moving man to sit still for long. Well, long enough to catch a cod or two, we hope, Joe. All the best to you and Beryl. I reckon you might see a few houses you'll recognise when you're travelling around.

Postscript

Joe sold me a big shed-load of HUGE Oregon timbers that he once used to move houses. The entire lot is now a wonderful addition to my own home – exposed for all to admire.

Outback and Beyond

MARGARET STUCHBERY

'SOMETIMES I SAT ON THE SANDHILLS AND LOOKED OUT ACROSS
THE SPARSE PLAIN. IT WAS LONELY AND YOU'D THINK OF HOME
— A THOUSAND MILES AWAY TO THE SOUTH.'

'It was an adventure, I always loved the bush, especially the outback.'

We were sitting in a home in Bendigo, looking out across a private pond with a pair of black ducks feeding and wandering the pond with half a dozen ducklings a few weeks old. Her home is in a private court with just a few other homes adjoining the large pond with waterlilies just coming into full bloom. The pond is surrounded by tall eucalypt trees. A private haven that many people would enjoy.

Margaret Stuchbery (née Dow) placed a cuppa on the table next to two plate-loads of dry biscuits with toppings and another plate of cake. Her lovely new home is filled with her craftwork, ranging from dozens of award-winning porcelain dolls in glass cabinets to artwork on walls. Even the three plates on the table before me she painted with beautiful art. She showed me one of the bedspreads she was knitting and some of her pastel art.

This is a lady who has seen a lot of life in her nearly 80 years. Her surroundings weren't always so stylish. She remembers other days when money and comforts weren't readily at hand. In her twilight years now she is settled and content, but not idle. She has survived two heart attacks and a bypass operation, but she is still full of living, and has plenty to keep her going. There's kids, grandkids and a multitude of things to do.

I wrote about her husband Allenby and two sons Ray and David in two of my books, *More Beaut Utes* and *Beaut Utes 3*. They are an interesting family.

She was born in the city but became a lover of the outback in her early years. 'I was born in Moreland, a Melbourne suburb. Have an older sister Eve, 81, in Sydney and younger sister Helen, 77, near Port Lincoln. Dad came from Broken Hill, married Mum in Port Adelaide. He was a returned World War I veteran, and had itchy feet. He worked on the railways. I was born in 1923. We moved from Melbourne to Queenstown, Tasmania, for about three years when I was real small, then to Adelaide. Dad had a hard time getting work, but eventually in 1929, he got a station worker job on Billila station on the Darling River near Wilcannia, where my grandfather was a rouseabout, and my grandmother was a cook.'

Memories obviously came flooding back when talking of Billila, as she laughed. 'Us girls always got into much mischief on the Darling. One day, however, the three of us were playing along the banks, and the oldest, Eve, wanted to gather some bluebells from down near the water. There were heaps up on the bank but she wanted different ones. I got sick of it, and pushed her into the river. The only thing that saved her from drowning were her neck-to-knee silk bloomers that blew up with air when she fell in, and we were able to pull her out. That was the final straw for my parents, so the two older ones, Eve and me, were sent to Gran's in Goodwood, Adelaide, to go to school there. Later at 13 I was sent to Goodwood Girls High School, but then in 1938 Dad got a job on the Commonwealth Railways at a small place between Port Pirie and Port Augusta, a railway siding called Winninowie, just five houses, 15 miles south of Port Augusta. From our front door you could see the Flinders Ranges, and from the back door Spencer Gulf. We did school by correspondence which came from Sydney.'

When she was just 16 Margaret Dow answered an ad in a newspaper, and by putting her age up, landed a job as a governess on Henbury Station, 75 miles south-west of Alice Springs in the Northern Territory. She went up on the old *Ghan* train. Alice Springs in 1940 was just a small dusty town in the middle of Australia.

'I think having lived on Billila conditioned me to later life in the Northern Territory. Henbury Station was pretty isolated. We had no vehicles on the property, just horses. The mail came by camel train once a month. It cost £10 for a car to come out from Alice Springs. It was a big cattle station. All the workers were Aborigines.

'They did all the stock work, broke in horses and looked after cattle. All the staff at the homestead also were Aborigines. Apart from the Draper family I was the only white employed there.

'Mr and Mrs Draper were the managers, who had four kids. The eldest was a bit of a pain. He offered to buy me a kitchen stove if I married him. Then there was 14-year-old Bob who was a little devil, Wanda was 7 years old, a lovely little kid, and Clare the baby was about two or three. My job was to supervise the correspondence school for the kids. After I left they wrote to me and asked would I consider coming back to work for them and young Bob would have to go to boarding school if I couldn't come back and supervise him. Boarding school was what he needed.

'I had my 17th birthday on Henbury. At the time the famous Reverend Flynn, who started the Flying Doctors Service, was there with his wife. I remember we were having the evening meal, and he looked across the table and said to me, "Miss Dow, you don't look old enough to be a governess." Mrs Draper, the manager's wife cut in and said, "I assure you she is, Reverend Flynn." She didn't know I wasn't.' Mrs Stuchbery gives a good-hearted laugh. 'I often wonder whatever happened to them all after I left.

'Reverend Flynn often called in and stayed on the station. He was a lovely old man, so natural. He just loved the outback and the people. We also had Alf Traegar who invented the pedal wireless, and Reverend Fred MacKay, Reverend Partridge and Reverend Albrecht all call in.

'Mrs Draper mollycoddled me and we got on well. I don't know how she put up with it out there. She did nothing; it was all done for her, she only had her kids. However, not long after I arrived everyone – family and staff – came down with measles one by one and she looked after all of us.

'We had one luxury, a kerosene fridge, and sometimes Mrs

Draper would make ice cream. The staff at the homestead included mission trained black housegirl Lorna and her black helper was Amy. And the black cook was a big fat lady called Alisha. She was a very good cook too.

'I loved them all. The girls at the homestead were great. The stockmen, too, were just big kids, laughing all the time. No way was there any alcohol problem in those days with them. They were good hard workers. There was one old black stockman Nahti, and he said I was the "proper pretty one". I was pale, delicate and with auburn hair. Finally I woke up he might have thoughts, so I had a lock put on my bedroom door.

'The girls did all the washing and ironing and always looked after me. With them you had a friend for life. The boys would kill meat for the station and cut it up and put it in the meat house. We'd have fresh meat for a few days, then it'd be salted and we lived on that for weeks on end. We even had goat for a change.

'The drinking water for the homestead was piped from the Finke River. It was very muddy water and at first I wouldn't drink it, only in a hot cup of tea, but eventually I got used to it. If you wanted a bath at night, that muddy water was pumped up from the Finke at midday, and it was so hot from the pipes you'd leave it until night when it had cooled.

'When I first went there the flies were so bad if a fly fell into the tea I'd throw it out. After a while, though, I got used to just fishing the flies out of the tea and continuing drinking. The flies were shocking.

'Sometimes I sat on the sandhills and looked out across the sparse plain. It was lonely and you'd think of home – a thousand miles away to the south, but you got over it.

You knew you couldn't go home until the end of the year.

'But really, I loved it up there. And I've always had a soft spot for the outback. Only reason I came home was my father wouldn't allow me to stay on as the Japs had bombed Darwin and he was afraid it wouldn't be safe.

'Winter we had white frost and summer we had blistering heat, but I liked the fresh air. The house was built of stone so it was cool in summer.

I used to get up about 7 each morning. School started at 8.30am. We had a proper self-contained school hut away from the house. It had tables and chairs and we had a proper school routine and timetable to stick to. The correspondence lessons came by mail and there would be a certain amount of time they had to work through them and then we'd send them back on the next mail. Mail was once a month.

'We stopped for morning tea and went to the house then back until lunchtime and worked through until 3.30pm when school finished. We had afternoon tea and then time was your own until dinner time. Kids loved to ride donkeys.

'At night we would listen to all the station news on the pedal wireless. Every station had a certain time to come on and give their news, details of what was happening, etc. Everyone reported in each day. You sort of got to know people through the pedal wireless. Other times at night we listened to an old gramophone and played old cowboy records.

'Five miles from the homestead was Henbury Meteorite Crater, but would you believe I never even got to see it. In fact, I didn't leave the property for the first six months. My pay was 18 shillings and sixpence a week which included my accommodation and food.

'When I first left the station it was to go to Erldunda station about 70 miles away. They had visitors from Melbourne and they sent a car from their station to pick us all up. I even ordered a long gown from Adelaide. I ordered it over the pedal wireless and it arrived when the mail came. It was a nice break, we danced to a gramophone.

'One thing I remember, and what a mistake. Gus Elliott was the camel driver who brought the mail once a month. He told us of this Aboriginal painter at Hermannsburg. Everyone was very impressed with what he was doing. He said we could buy small paintings for 10 shillings. But we felt we couldn't afford them. The painter was an Aborigine called Albert Namatjira. Wish I had some of his paintings now.'

In recent times Mrs Stuchbery visited Alice Springs and like most tourists bought a series of small Albert Namatjira prints of his paintings.

'I met many other people up there. One of the first stations out from Alice was Renners Rock, where Alf Butler and Bob Buck lived. Bob Buck is remembered as being involved with Bob Lasseter of Lasseter's Reef fame. We also had regular visits from Tempy Downs station.

'The Inland Mission padres often came through. Hermannsburg Mission in those days had a good vegetable garden. The missionaries would come to Henbury with nice vegetables to give out. We never ever got any, it always went to the Aborigines.

'When the well-known Reverend Albrecht retired he bought a property at Sellecks Beach near Adelaide, and my parents lived there also, and I remember going around to see him and have afternoon tea with him.'

Muffy, the lovable 12-year-old little dog, interrupts proceedings and lets us know she wants some cake or biscuit. She is given a dog biscuit instead. Then she is let outside on the back verandah. 'We go for a walk every day and she's pretty fit for her age,' says Mrs Stuchbery.

Anyway, finally it came to an end. The Japanese had commenced bombing raids on Darwin, and although she was on a station many hundreds of miles south, her father felt it was too dangerous, as word at the time was the Japs could invade Australia. As a returned soldier from World War I, her father no doubt had visions of war still vivid in his memory. His daughter was coming home to the safety of the family.

'I got on a train for home, but it broke down at Maree and we were delayed there for many hours. There was nothing much there and we only got some scraps to eat. Finally, we got going again and it was a stop at Quorn that changed things. I liked the look of Quorn and I walked into a shop and got myself a job. It was a mixed business and I ended up staying there for the next twelve to eighteen months I guess. I served in the shop and also packed orders in boxes to go north. I didn't know it at the time but I had in fact packed two that went to my future husband Allenby. He was just 19 and working on the Commonwealth Railways at places like William Creek, Edwards Creek and places up north repairing engines.

'He came to Port Augusta from Portland on loan to the Railways, during the war. Anyway I later landed a job in about 1942 in a mixed business in Port Augusta. Allenby then lived around the corner from the shop and he walked past each day and came in to buy a milkshake.

'During the war I decided to join the Air Force and entered

the WRAAF and did six weeks of rookie training at Victor Harbour, south of Adelaide. And I trained as an office orderly. Then I was posted to Melbourne, where I lived with some WRAAF girls in a mansion in Toorak. We travelled to Albert Park each day to the barracks. Was in Medical Statistics, coding medical papers for when RAAF crews come down home from the islands. Every illness had a code number and we did all the paperwork. Later the group was disbanded and I could have applied to be sent anywhere in Australia, but I went back to South Australia and worked at a RAAF office in Adelaide. We then regrouped to a base office in the grounds of the Adelaide hospital, and I stayed there until the end of the war.

'Six weeks after my discharge, I married Allenby at Scot's Church, Adelaide on 3 November 1945. We had a month's honeymoon at Port Lincoln. As the war was finished Allenby was only on loan to the Commonwealth Railways. A friend of his lived in Bendigo, and we came to live with them for a while.

'I, however, was now pregnant with David and was sick so went to Adelaide to the family to be looked after. Allenby then bought the place where we would live for the rest of our married life. We settled into it in 1946 and were there over fifty years, until I sold it and the blocks of land a couple of years ago and moved here.

'Back then the original old home was one built in the 1800s and just had wallpaper over old hessian. We got two calves, raised them and when we sold them one paid the rates on the house, and the other paid the registration on the car – an old 1934 Ford V8 ute. Allenby was back working for the Victorian Railways but resigned and got a job at the ordinance factory in

1948. He started as a boilermaker tradesman and retired due to ill-health as an A Grade Foreman. He died in 1993.

'Anne was born in 1948, Ray in 1952 and Harry in 1957. In the 1960s I went back to work when I was in my forties, first as home supervisor at a nursing home, then I was offered a job at the Bendigo Base Hospital in medical records initially, then I went into admissions, and then casualty reception. I thoroughly enjoyed working there and I learnt a lot. Finally I retired in 1988.'

All the family were into athletics for many years. Husband Allenby was as keen as their three boys, and as 'Anne was a tomboy and wanted to be in it', Mrs Stuchbery decided to start the South Bendigo Women's Athletic Club, and did it for many years. 'We lived there, practically. Training about three times a week. Then competitions at the weekend, and they even came around to our house to practise. Shot-put, javelin, discus throwing, hammer.'

As you can imagine, there would be no idle retirement for Mrs Stuchbery. No one in the Stuchbery family sits still for long. As a very good seamstress she kept busy, and it was time to branch out into a new interest as well.

'I went to a pottery class for adults, and later an art camp at Portland. I then learnt enamelling and copper work. We even went up to Mt Isa at one stage to teach some nuns how to do copper art work.

'Then I did a silversmith jewellery course at the Bendigo University and got a "D". I was horrified and threw the report in the bin. I found out later the D was for "Distinction",' laughed Mrs Stuchbery.

'Then I did a creative living course studying acrylic painting, then another course on doing pastels, and then a course on china painting and ten years ago I learnt about porcelain dolls. I've done many dolls over the years.'

She pointed to a doll sitting on the side table. 'That one is ready for the next doll show in February. I donate every year, and funds go to Kids with Cancer and Bone Marrow charity. I've lost count how many dolls I've made.' She casually mentions she's won a few times, and I saw ribbons and awards including a recent one Best Senior 2000, and more. At one show she took out first prize in three separate sections.

But it's time to move on and she says she's 'now in semi retirement' but she adds she'd 'like to get back into doing pastel drawing again. We couldn't afford any of this when I was a kid. I learnt to sew and knit but we didn't have a lot of money. Mum was good at sewing. I made all the kids' clothes for many years.'

She still makes dozens of fancy bride's horseshoes for people, and also took up doing beaded work and showed me a fine detailed example of her work. 'I find I don't have the patience much any more. If it doesn't work out the first time it hits the bin.'

She still travels herself and was in Darwin recently and hopes to complete other planned trips. She has also just bought a brand new car.

Reading has taken Mrs Stuchbery to many places also. She loves biographies, and any book to do with the outback and bush. She loves adventure. She just finished reading Di Morrisey's *Kimberley Sun*. She says, 'You don't have to be lonely when you're alone – if you've got a good book. To lose yourself in a book gives you a love of reading.'

How would she sum up her life?

'I've been lucky – I've been blessed.'

Ned Kelly's Mate

GARY DEAN

'WE'VE SENT REPLICA KELLY GANG SUITS OF ARMOUR ALL OVER
THE GLOBE. ONE THING I'VE LEARNT THROUGH RESEARCHING
HISTORY — IT'S A SMALL WORLD.'

If Ned Kelly, our most famous bushranger and Australia's last outlaw, was ever to miraculously reappear in life, one of the men he would probably want to track down is Gary Dean of Glenrowan, to get some royalties from all the Ned Kelly memorabilia that Gary has sold over the years (along with hundreds of others, me included, as I wrote two books on bushrangers.)

In Gary Dean's case, he'd probably want to sign up as Ned's business manager, and the two of them could go off and make more money than Ned ever did robbing stagecoaches, squatters and banks during the 1870s.

Gary Dean lives and breathes Ned Kelly. He has made Ned his business and his life. We first met at a Ned Kelly weekend of lectures in Wangaratta in 1980, 100 years after Ned was hanged in Old Melbourne Gaol. I was just finishing off my first bushranger book and at the time lived and breathed bushrangers too. Anyone who had a historical interest in those days knew how obsessed I was with writing history, and books on bushrangers in my collection amount to not dozens but hundreds.

My writing career changed and evolved and after about 20 years or more of researching bushrangers, and after publishing a second book on the subject, I finally went in a different direction. But Gary Dean's interest in bushrangers deepened and he went into it with more gusto and eventually into the business of bushrangers, but particularly Ned Kelly.

He owns and runs Glenrowan Cobb & Co, an Australiana gift store specialising in Ned Kelly, and also has a Ned Kelly bushranging memorabilia museum downstairs. He is also an avid researcher and writer of Ned's life, with a good memory for dates and details. Not everyone agrees with his research but then most historians have their critics of some sort.

Gary was born in Mooroopna to an irrigation farming family. He moved to south of Glenrowan in 1967 with his parents to run 1000 acres, a sheep property with '1200 first-cross ewes and Poll Dorset rams, 500 Merino wethers and 30 cattle'. They completed all-new fencing and finally sold out in 1981. The stock were on agistment to fatten up, then were sold to the Middle East, and that way they made better money than normal farming.

Gary then went to Beechworth where he did an adult apprenticeship in conjunction with Oakleigh TAFE Horticulture School. Sixteen started the course and eleven passed in two years instead of the normal four, Gary included. The following year he became a qualified landscaper. He worked as a foreman with Wangaratta City Council, and ended up as Superintendent of Parks & Gardens for five years.

In 1984 he opened stage one of his shop at Glenrowan, and had three ladies working it during the week, and ran it himself at weekends with his wife.

In 1989 he built the rest of his shop at Glenrowan. He divorced in 1990 and finally starting working it himself full time in 1990 and also extended the shop. He opened the museum section in 1992. His new partner in life, Allison Keir, a psychologist, also has a connection to Glenrowan. 'Her grandparents owned the Glenrowan Hotel and her father was born at the foot of the stairs.'

Gary for many years was an avid bottle collector, and has one of the largest collections in Victoria, some 9000 bottles, even dating back to 17th-century Chinese burial urns, old opium pipes and such. He spent years collecting and digging around the old gold towns like Beechworth, and most of his collection dates back to before 1880. He searched many old town sites as well as old goldfields towns.

'It was through searching for bottles that I learnt a lot of history, where the old horse changing stations were, etc.,' says Gary. 'A property we bought once was owned by one of Ned Kelly's uncles, Albert Griffiths, and that got me interested in the Kelly Gang as far back as 1967,' he continues, stroking his long Ned-type beard.

'I was always active in the district: I met many descendants of Ned and became interested, and we talked and became good friends of the family. I heard all sorts of stories, including one about a suit of armour that was dragged from a dam in 1943 near Glenrowan by an old neighbour, Chris Iskov. I got talking to the old fella and he told me about the armour.

'The first ten years when I was researching I never checked records, I just talked to the old blokes of the district at tennis matches or at bushfires. I've had a few fiery confrontations but allies jumped to my defence. The Griffith and Lloyd families are descendants of the Kellys and the subject for many years was taboo; they'd just frighten off or offend people, as the memory was too painful. Over the years I've spoken to hundreds of descendants of the Kellys, the police involved, and other people from town.'

Over the years of my own research into bushrangers, I can say that the Ned Kelly story is a mixture of wonderful inspiring historical interesting fact, myth, concocted bullshit and totally absurd allegations. I lost count of how many people I've met who say they are related to Ned, or their great grandpappy was the other unknown gang member or their great grandmother used to date Ned when she was a girl. One bloke told me his grandfather once arrested Ned. His grandfather was born in 1901, some twenty-one years after Ned was hanged!

There is no doubt Ned's story is an interesting one, one of the most interesting in Australian criminal and social history. I believe we have just scratched the surface of what will be found on Ned and his mates, but unfortunately there is more and more fiction being spread and many of the prime sources are now gone.

When I wrote my *100 Australian Bushrangers* and updated *Stand & Deliver*, I spent years searching through prison records and official government department records. It was there I located many prison photographs never published before of bushrangers – thrilling finds.

During that research I also located a huge amount of new records, particularly on bushranger Harry Power, the man who taught Ned, and much of that material I allowed noted historian Ian Jones to use in his best-selling book *Ned Kelly*. Ian, a friend of many years, also agrees we have only started to find information and Ian has been researching Ned longer than probably anyone else in Australia.

One aspect that is now coming to the fore and which may prove very interesting in the Kelly case is DNA testing. Gary Dean is right into this form of research, and hopes to prove and solve conclusively many mysteries of the Ned Kelly story. Whilst DNA analysis has become a phenomenal resource now used worldwide to solve identities of long-dead and living people, there is another aspect of Gary's research that may cause some scepticism. He is a water diviner and has been for some thirty years. Now he uses that old craft, which has been employed around the world for generations, for another purpose. He uses it to find where bodies were buried and where building sites were.

'Divining enables us to make many more breakthroughs in research,' he says. 'The body has a magnetic field, 30 millivolts or less you cannot divine.' Gary says he works between 50–130 millivolts. 'Human remains have a magnetic field and the best tool for divining is a steel wire shape like the letter "L", either fencing wire or that from a coathanger.

'The divining,' he says, 'picks up holes dug and filled, where walls were, etc. Many people were buried in unmarked graves, particularly convicts, bushrangers and early pioneers.'

Gary's plotting of cemeteries includes many maps he's drawn up on computer and these are compared with previous drawings and known information. He continually is researching. He is now, with others, arranging exhumation of some of the graves for technical analysis, and this could be where science proves details of what have been, for generations, the unsolved mysteries.

'In exhuming a body we need permission of family descendants and the Health Department. To date one of four planned exhumations has been done, that of Charles Devine Tindall at Toowoomba, Queensland. He claimed to be Dan Kelly, and was said to have escaped the fire at Glenrowan and not died in the burning of the inn at the last stand where Ned was finally captured.' The testing is incomplete, but Gary says there was a consistent 'scar on the right cheek and he was the same height' as Dan. Further testing is still to be done and money is needed, as it isn't a cheap exercise.

Approval for sampling of two living relatives of Mrs Kelly (Ned's mother) has been given. DNA and y-chromosome testing has been conducted through Anatomical Sciences at Adelaide University and by a university in Canada.

There is no doubt DNA testing has and will continue to solve murders, unusual deaths and more as science develops. Police believe it is one of the greatest weapons to fight crime in the last century of forensic development. Whether it will solve many of the unanswered questions of the Kelly saga remains to be seen.

Gary is co-author of a number of books – *Ned & Others, Horsemen Bold, Harry Power, To Crack a Whip* – and has written in many other publications. He continues to research for future books.

Over the next couple of years he intends doing a lot of work to ensure he has the largest website devoted to Ned Kelly: www.nedkellysworld.com.au. He intends developing his museum further, displaying many items from the Kelly story. 'The museum is underground – it's fireproof, earthquake proof, has security doors and 24-hour electronic surveillance.'

Gary wants to find more time for research – he says he has so many leads still to follow. The phone never stops ringing while you talk to Gary, someone chasing information or wanting to pass on some lead to him. He always has a yarn.

I have an amusing vision of Ned Kelly sitting somewhere in another life, adding up all who have profited from his life, keeping a tally and one day calling, guns in hand, demanding his share. If he calls on Gary it will be like looking in a mirror with their beards the most dominant features.

Gary's store sells roughly 7000 individual items for tourists, some 180 of those being specific Ned Kelly items. Everything from key-rings to mugs, T-shirts, books, postcards, badges, fridge magnets, clocks, wall plaques, videos, plates and wind chimes. All jam-packed into a store for the devoted Kellyana devotee or tourist collector in general. 'Something to tempt everybody,' says Gary.

One interesting item that sells well is the replica suit of armour, full copies of what the Ned Kelly Gang wore in the gunfight with police. 'A local blacksmith bloke makes them for me, one sort is $450 and the other $1100. He makes them using the full weights just like the Kelly armour and also half weights. We also have one worth $8500 – a real work of art.'

Gary is constantly asked to assist in all sorts of Kelly work. He has helped set up bars wanting an Australiana theme, and his replicas of full-size Kelly armour suits have been sold all over the world.

'From Dubai to Dublin, Ireland – we've also sent replica Kelly Gang suits of armour to Los Angeles, New York, London, two to Canada, three to New Zealand, two to Germany – and even one to a national bank in Shanghai, China.'

In a joint project of the Rural City of Wangaratta and the State Government Glenrowan now has a strategic plan for future development. A $40,000 blueprint has been developed, and large grants of money will assist projects in stages. Glenrowan is now a heritage area – particularly the siege site where the Kellys' days of bushranging, bank robbing and such were brought to an end.

There are plans to rebuild the Glenrowan Inn, to what it was like in 1880 during the siege. 'Much of it depends on the people and what they want,' says Gary. 'The attitude from most is positive in Glenrowan now. For many years the subject of Ned was taboo and locals wouldn't allow anything to be done to remind the public of the story. But times have changed and the public have never gone away and continually want to see it all.

'There's often overseas tourists come in who have never heard of him, but many Irish people who know of Ned's Irish family connections come, and they always say when you come to Australia you "gotta go to Glenrowan". Many are very disappointed when there's "nothing to see" and all the buildings from the period are gone.'

In fact, I believe there was a concerted effort many years ago to obliterate all and anything connected to the Kellys. The pros and cons of the story were felt very deeply by both authorities and families for many generations, and persist today.

'I would get at least two or three people in here a week who say they have a connection to the Kellys,' says Gary. 'Stage one of the future for Glenrowan includes the closure of Siege Street, building footpaths, landscaping, car parks, etc. Stage two includes signage, promotion to get people to the town, self-guided tours, public amenities. Stage three could be a museum, a theatre, an interpretation centre, and more.'

Ned would be smiling, with government departments who spent so much money trying to arrest him now spending money to promote him. As Ned would say, 'Such is life.'

Doing research of any kind is fascinating, I've been doing it all my working life. Gary Dean has similarly found it interesting and I agree when he says: 'One thing I've learnt through historical research is it's a small world. In genealogy you learn so much – there's many connections. I've wanted to know the truth of the Kelly story, and the real joy is in the discovery – and sharing the discovery with other people. I have hardcore Kelly fanatics come here up to six times a year. We get an enormous number of people from all over the world. There's even a lady in Japan writing a book on Ned now.'

The many books on Ned include, in 2000, the fanciful novel by Peter Carey, *True History of the Kelly Gang.* Another in the long line of Kelly movies, based on a novel by Robert Drewe, was released in 2003.

And what of the people who are against Ned and all he meant? 'There two sorts: those who have never read anything or are descendants of police of the time.'

And finally, Gary's thoughts on the Kelly Gang?

'They were not all innocent, they were very hard done by; Ned was a product of his environment, and a hero to the underdog and the persecuted. The armour is the symbol of the Kelly legend.'

'Man Who Paints With Fire'

RON CLARKE
'I WANT TO BE THE REMBRANDT OF THIS FORM OF ART.'

Down in the Riverina
Where the Murrumbidgee flows
Beside the old Sturt Highway
Once used by Cobb & Co
In an old abandoned roadhouse
With his torch and sheets of iron
It's there that you'll find Clarkie
The man who paints with fire.

Jack Forrester

'They still call me a Pommie bastard when I walk down the street. I'm as much Australian as I'll ever be.

'Well, I am a genuine cockney, born in the heart of London in 1937. My great grandfather's family were coachbuilders in

Norwich. His name was Charlie Cobb. He became a rag 'n' bone man (a scrap-metal seller) in London. Don't worry about grand-father, he was just a factory worker, and then my father who was an engineer, he did everything and ended up a company director.

'Me, I left school at 15. It was thought I should get a trade and my Dad said, "Well, what do you want to be?" and I said, "I want to be just like you." He said, "I'll teach you to be a survivor." That's what he taught me – how to be a survivor. I was pretty close to my Dad.'

It was Australia Day 2002 – I'd been to the opening of the Shearer's Hall of Fame in Hay, New South Wales, and finished an interview for another book. It was in the garden of a private place that I saw a steam train steel sculpture and I asked the man where he got it.

When I found out it wasn't all that far away I knew I had to get there to interview the man. A few hours later, after a warm drive, I spotted the signs and pulled in to what looked like an abandoned motel, next to a roadhouse, near the junction of roads that led to Griffith or straight on to Narrandera.

One of the various signs says Ron Clarke – Metal Craftsman. That he is, and more.

Ron Clarke lives in a closed motel with his two sons, Bob, 39, and Ron junior, 36. And a huge pet bull that likes to be ridden. Dogs are also part of the family including one that let me know he wanted to rip my arm and leg off. Fortunately for me, he was tied to a chain. I made myself known to Ron and his boys and they welcomed me into their world. I had a tour of their business, and soon we were seated inside out of the heat.

'Dad had a contract with the J. Arthur Rank Movie studio in

England. He shifted, by low loader, a 25-ton treadmill from studio to studio when they were working on different films. Every time he went to the studio he'd give me a day off school because, he'd say, "Listen, son, you'll learn more than in school, so you're coming with me today, it'll open your mind."

'So I'd get to see the work on various sets, watching how artists painted huge stage sets. One movie I saw in the making was *Scott of the Antarctic*. I always did a lot of looking around, I learnt a hell of a lot, they way they stuck paint on. Then I had some art lessons for about two years, and the bloke who taught me, said to Dad, "Let him do his own thing, let him go." I was about 15.

'Dad was a brilliant artist – the most expressive hands. He had big hands and was into engineering, but he could also do intricate model carving. It was him who told me with paint to "be bold".

'I learnt more and then I did a lot of posters. Then painting things like bunches of fruit on the sides of greengrocer trucks, nudes on trucks. I used to paint a lot of horse teams like Cobb & Co and I sold many paintings.

'In 1951 we paid our fare to Australia and ended up at Port Kembla. We bought an old Reo truck and we lived in a tent right on Shellharbour. We had an ice run, carting to places like Windang and Primby.

'Between 1954 and 1957 I was driving trucks. I did contract work on a front-end loader at Picton for the Water Board. Later we got a parcel of land at Bargo. Things got really tough there.

'Dad heard about opal and how some Yank found huge pieces, so we threw everything on the truck and pissed off, just

before Christmas 1956. We got as far as Darling Point, and with no money looked around for a job.

'I got work driving a dozer for the Water Commission. Dad was a hydraulic engineer, but ended up working as a mechanic on draglines. We needed to get work on our own so we bought two old trucks on "grandmother terms – book it up to the Jews and let Christ pay for it".

'Then it was a two-year stint on trucks again, before we bought this land here at Waddi. It was the first bitumen road between Sydney and Adelaide, so we built the roadhouse that's next door and ran it for seven years, and we built the motel at the same time. Both Dad and Mum were with us all the time. They're both dead now. Dad taught my son how to be a mechanic.'

Clarkie pulls beer from his large commercial fridge. He fills a jug. This is no ordinary beer, it's Clarkie's special homebrew. 'Now you'll stay for some lunch, mate,' he says, and so I share time with him and his two sons out the back under a large shadeclothed verandah. Dogs wander around and plop down beside us. It is much cooler here than outside.

'I was always interested in silhouettes; they are like mime – tell a message, a powerful one. I could never leave a bit of ply alone, I'd always get a fretsaw out and make a silhouette of something.

'I was working for a farmer – he was buying up farms and I'd make a gate sign for each one. I always put some sort of silhouette on top of the sign.

'It was about 1983 or '84. I'd grabbed a piece of steel and with the oxy made a tractor from front on. I said to my son, Ron junior, "Want to come on out and see what I've made?"

He looked at it, and said, "You gotta do a tractor side-on." He was pretty dismissive about it. The hair stood up on the back of my neck, and I thought, geez that's great. There was a painting on the wall of a horseman and I thought, I can do that.

'In 1985 I was driving trucks, as the motel wasn't making money, and Dad was dying at the time – tough times. I was always very close to Dad, so much so they called us the "Clarke Brothers". He loved Aussie beer, Dad.

'It was Dad who taught me how to use an oxy. I remember when I said "Come outside, I want to show you what I've made". He looked at this sculpture and just said "That's real good" – I was rapt. He died a few days later. He was 72.

'Finally I decided I can't just always have one foot on safe ground, I had to get back to working for myself. The first real sculpture I made was a horse team, and the boss at an engineering place asked how much I wanted for it, and I said 20 bucks. He said that was too cheap and gave me 50 dollars for it – my first sale. He also said to me, "What are you doing driving trucks?" And so that was the way it happened.

'I was obsessed with learning how to master it. I'd been working all day on trucks, and all night long in my sleep I'd be cutting out bits of steel. I was so frustrated. I had one sculpture collapse but it's never happened since. I eventually knew I had to get the confidence, and always had to think ahead as I worked. Now I don't hesitate, I just get it done.

'It took me twelve months to get the big breakthrough, and completely understand what to do and how to do it. Now, though, I'm 66 years old and getting better at it!

'With this work it's different, there's no half-tones like photos. I've got two colours to work with – black steel and the holes (white). The holes become the chrome, the shine on paint you'd normally see in a photo, but in actual fact it's just where I've cut out a piece of steel. There's something extra – know when to stop, before it collapses.

'I'm pretty well self-taught with no training. The bolder I got, the better I got and the better the pieces got. Many people get shit from the tip, weld it together and call it art. This is brand new BHP steel.

'My philosophy is I'll only refuse cash when the government stops printing it. It's been a struggle, but I love it. This is the first time in my life doing what I really love, instead of working a "normal" job. I was always looking for the opportunity.

'There's only one Rembrandt. I want to be the Rembrandt of this form of artwork. I don't care who takes it up, but I want to be the best at it.'

There are now many fine examples of Clarkie's steel work scattered around. At Hilton, New South Wales, he did the Kidman Way sign; at Jugiong, a large sign to get people to come to the town; in Strathmerton, a bakery sign; at Junee, a shire grader given to a man who'd worked for them for forty years; at Leeton – the Vietnam Veterans Memorial – a helicopter; a large wheat header at Henty; a big Mack truck for the Brisbane Expo. He's also made the winning post sculptures at the Narrandera and Carrathool racetracks.

'I've made dozens and dozens of station property gates and farm signs all over the place. Some of my sculptures have ended up in places like Tulsa, USA; Canada, Ireland, England.

'Someone always gets a nookie because of my work,' laughs Clarkie, as he's sure that when someone takes a piece of his work home, a wife or husband is more than happy.

'I worked three years on my own and now my two sons have been in the business with me, and I'm passing on to them just like my Dad did with me.'

By far the biggest job Clarkie has done so far, with sons by his side, was for the Sydney headquarters of Gough & Gilmore Caterpillar (CAT) in Parramatta. It measures 30 feet by 12 feet and is mounted on a wall of the main building.

I could spend a great deal of time with Clarkie, he's an interesting, talented but very down-to-earth man. But for now, the time had finally come for me to say farewell. It's been an interesting time. A Ron Clarke sculpture is ordered for my collection, and I promise to return.

The sign at the front of the property says, *Ron Clarke, Steel Craftsman*. But that is wrong, and I think he needs to change it. It should read: Ron Clarke – Master Steel Craftsman.

Postscript

I have since returned to see Ron and his sons. Word has spread and they are extremely busy making all sorts of steel sculptures for a growing clientele.

'I'm very contented with the way things are going,' says Ron. 'The boys have really taken it on, which is good as the art won't die with me. We now make handmade, specialised artwork. I'm happy to be freelance: the struggle is to keep it out of the hands of managers. Here you deal with me direct.'

Tantanoola Traveller

ROBERT 'NED' HUNT

'WHILE TRAVELLING I REALISED YOU CAN'T JUST KEEP HAVING GOOD
TIMES ALL THE TIME – IT WAS HARD TO PUT UP WITH ALL THAT
GOOD WEATHER – AND BESIDES, I MISSED MY SHED.'

If you don't like pine trees by the thousands, then don't drive
between Mt Gambier and Millicent in South Australia. Me,
I love the look, smell and touch of eucalypts. I hate bloody
pine trees! But pine trees are a necessity for timber; they
keep many people employed in the timber industry directly
and many others indirectly – everyone from truck drivers,
mechanics, suppliers to manufacturers and much more. But
I still hate bloody pine trees. At least every eucalypt looks
different. Pine plantations look and feel like ecological deserts
– dark canopy with nothing underneath but pine needles. Still,
Mt Gambier and district is a lovely place.

For me, there was an interesting highlight to travelling this
road. And an excuse to have a break from looking at pines –
and that's how I met 'Ned'.

He's got the disease just like me – *travelitis*. Listening to him talk of his love of travel was just like listening to myself. The disease is almost a 'persistent bug'. I've had it for over 30 years, and getting worse. Mine is incurable and inoperable.

Robert 'Ned' Hunt is a man who'd work at anything. It was his sign on the side of the road and the ancient looking buildings that caught my eye, and screeching to a halt and doing a u-turn I saw something in his yard that I wanted a closer look at to buy – a windmill.

I love windmills. Unfortunately I ended up not buying this one: I wanted a Southern Cross windmill and this was a Bryan Bros, and although a good one, good price with heaps of spare head and tails, it wasn't a Southern Cross.

Anyway, we had a talk, and finally we were seated in his kitchen, after he'd taken me on a tour of his shop and shed and the wonderful old pub out the front.

Ned, as most people call Robert, says the pub was built in the 1800s but closed in 1864. Ned's business is called *Caves Secondhand*, which is on the Princes Highway between Mount Gambier and Millicent in South Australia.

Robert Hunt was born in the same year as me, 1951, in Millicent. We also share another thing, we both have bone diseases. Mine is Pagets, his he had by the time he was 5 years old – osteomyelitis. His bone disease spread from his leg to his arm and shoulder. He was in hospital for twelve months and had ongoing treatment right up until about fourteen years ago when a local doctor got him into a hyperbaric centre in Adelaide.

'I had treatment for two hours daily for thirty days. They put you into a chamber and take the pressure down to 18 metres, just like they do when they work with underwater divers with the bends. They pump in pure oxygen, and it goes to the weakest part of the body and opens the blood vessels and promotes healing. I had two sessions daily and was "brought to the surface" over a half-hour period. Now I don't have pain and it's probably cured, but I'm not certain.

'I left school and went to work in the building trade for five years with my father who is a carpenter/building contractor. Then when I was 21, I left and went to Adelaide for twelve months working as a shed hand for Loys Soft Drinks, then back home for two years between 1975 and 1977 at the paper mill.'

Ned moved to Tantanoola in the late seventies and lived on the block in a caravan with no water and no electricity. He built a room.

'The old pub was built by William Wilson and his three brothers in the 1800s to service the area. In 1864 the pub closed as the railways went through Tantanoola township a few kilometres away. Later people lived in it, and for about ten years it was empty when my uncle bought it, then my father bought it off him and then I built the current house in the mid eighties when Sue moved in. She's a clerk for an accountant in Millicent.'

Rob and Sue settled in to make it home. Rob started a bike hire business as a way of teaching the local kids how to ride. He expanded into beach buggies and mini bikes with sidecars. After a couple of years he went on to continue working for himself at whatever he could. Tiling, odd jobs, even security guard on a construction site.

'Between September 1990 and August 1991, we went around Australia, and were just on the Nullarbor when the petrol prices went up due to the Gulf War. Anyway, we headed off for about

twelve months and went to Perth, up the west coast, Wittenoom, Hammersleys, Gibb Road, Mitchell Falls, to Darwin, Kakadu. We did all the "touristy things". Then we came home via Alice Springs, Glen Helen, followed the Finke River to Kings Canyon, Ayers Rock, Chambers Pillar, Dalhousie Springs, Woomera, Andamooka. We didn't see much of the highway at all. We had a car-top camper on top of a Rodeo 4x4 1600 dual cab which was on petrol and gas. She was a bloody beauty. It had been Dad's for ten years with only 50,000km on it when I got it.'

Home again, they ran his father's caravan park for two years. Wally was born in 1919 and he and wife Millie are now retired. Rob has two brothers: Ron, 55, who works in caravan sales and service, and Alan (known as Kirk) 63, a carpenter and builder. Rob and Sue lived at the caravan park as they had rented their home out.

'In 1994 we just packed up and headed off again. Mildura, Broken Hill, Wilcannia, Bourke, Cunnamulla, Charlieville, Longreach, Cloncurry, Mt Isa, Normanton, Carumba, Cairns, and then to the tip of Cape York via Cooktown and the Daintree. We followed the telegraph line towards Bamaga.

'We got a job on a pearl farm on Roko Island for three months. A magnificent place. Me doing maintenance work and cutting pearl shells, Sue doing sorting and grading pearls.'

They left the island but returned again after Rob worked in a garage which he didn't like. Eventually it was time to head south, but they only got as far as Townsville where he says 'the temperature plummeted to the mid 20s so we headed north again and west.' Finally they made their way back to Brisbane, Nimbin, to the coast and down to Sydney, Bathurst, Orange,

Parkes, Forbes, Cowra, Canberra, Cooma, Batlow, Corryong, Gundagai, Albury, along the Murray River, Shepparton, Echuca, Mildura, into South Australia and back home. In all they'd been away well over twelve months and arrived home for Christmas 1995.

'While travelling I realised you can't just keep having good times all the time – it was hard to put up with all that good weather – and besides, I missed my shed.

'We were going into second-hand shops all the time, and we decided to have a go at it, and we still had a bit of cash left over, so we bought a new shed. It took me two years to get it finished and all set up. We opened just before Christmas 1998. Good way to get rid of old stuff here and we bought bits and pieces. We sell about 50/50 to locals and to tourists from all over the world. Lots of English people, few South Americans, lots of Israelis. Everything goes in cycles. Everything sells – it's just a matter of time.'

It's quiet in winter but summer is good; depends on weather. We sell everything from windmills, to crockery, books, furniture, old curios. Rake hoes, thicknessers, all sorts of tail-lights, farm machinery. I like the "boy's toys" – motors, tools, outboard motors – shed stuff.'

Rob buys at clearing sales and travels as far as Adelaide to find the right piece for his shop. He also takes a bit of stuff on consignment. 'When I first started I lost my own shed for storage space, and I still miss it.

'Our generation can just about build anything, but we are unemployable. I have a go at anything. You must turn your hand to anything.'

The business is now up for sale. Nice home, 10 acres on two

5-acre titles of land, pub, shop – the lot. About 2000 cars a day pass the place.

Yep, you guessed it – they want to travel.

'As soon as it's sold we're going. Don't know where, probably to England to see a mate first and then more travelling around. The place also has 3-phase power and an underground water bore.'

So good luck to them – I'm sure they'll survive, they are old hands at travelling now. I bet Rob will miss his shed, though.

'I'll sell most of my stuff as well, we'll just travel, play it by ear – something always turns up.'

Three Women of substance

MAUREEN TIMSON
MARY JOSEPHINE O'CONNELL
CECILIA O'CONNELL

'I'M A SLIGHTLY BENT HERBALIST. ALL THE LOCAL KIDS USED TO
COME AROUND — THEY THOUGHT I WAS A WITCH.'

It seems most appropriate that in order to get to Maureen's place you go on a rough dirt road past the local cemetery gates, along a track that says 'no through road'. The further you go the more it narrows, past remains of old stone walls of the goldfields era.

The track is overgrown with eucalypts, wattles and a variety of native bush, ideal surroundings for a lady who specialises in many elements of the natural world. This is a bush retreat to Maureen and Dave Timson's liking. 'When we first walked onto this block we knew this was where we wanted to be. In fact, years earlier when we first met we said we wanted to live in a hut in the bush with no running water, no light and an outside loo, and that's exactly what happened here.'

Next to the old place, though, is a 'nearing completion, paid cash as we went' two-storey home of brick, bush stone and slate, all built by Dave and family. It is home, and harmony is a word that comes to mind.

They moved here permanently in 1988. Dave is an architectural draftsman, Maureen a herbalist. Up on top of the bush-covered hill from their home is a two-room cottage. One room is Dave's drafting office, and the other is Maureen's studio.

When I first met her she was a lady who could barely walk, even with the aid of a walking frame or two crutches. Now with two replaced hips she is a new woman. She has just a bit of a limp. Dave nicknamed her Snails, 'because she is slow and always leaves a mess behind'. He adds, 'The kids may have thought she was a witch, but she's a white one, a good one.' She takes his weird bush humour with a laugh.

Maureen comes from an interesting background. She is a direct descendant of Irishman Daniel O'Connell, a lawyer educated in England, who was known as The Liberator. The family property is Derrynane in County Clare. The family came to Australia when two brothers in the family were shot and the family forced off the property.

Born in 1939, Maureen has always had an interesting life. Some of her childhood was spent living in the experimental community Maryknoll (see Maureen's mother's story below). At the age of 16 she went nursing at Sacred Heart Hospital in Melbourne and finished three years later in 1958. However, it was the pressure of seeing so many baby deaths that confirmed to Maureen she wanted a total change, so got a job to help set up the first colour printing department at Kodak in Abbotsford, where her uncle worked. Whilst she knew nothing of the industry, she soon learnt, as 'lacky' for two men. She became the first operator doing computer printing, coding of colour, contrast, density. She did a lot of special computer coding work. She worked there for about six years from the late 1950s and into the sixties.

However, her family thought it was time Maureen also went to finishing school. So she went studying and to lectures at TaCregan, a finishing school in Hawthorn, with twenty-three others in a Tudor house that was originally brought out on a ship from England. It was there she met up with Dave and they married in 1961. They set up home in the hills out from Melbourne 'when Ferntree Gully was just bush tracks'. They stayed for 27 years before moving to their shack shangrila in the bush.

They had five children, now 'all extremely creative' people. Michelle, 40, is a carer and writer; Lisa, 38, an art director in film media; Matthew, 36, a film director with Channel 9; Justin, 34, musician and teacher, and didgeridoo maker in England; and Nicholas, 32, self-employed with a business called 'Climb Access' (repair and maintenance on big buildings) and also an inventor.

Maureen ended up in a TAFE college teaching everything from survival skills to soap-making; spinning and weaving to small business setting-up. Much of her time in the eighties was spent working with unemployed youth. She also worked in Community Houses teaching herbal information like plant identification and plant uses. These were skills she's picked up over many years herself as well as some form of natural talent for it. It was also a handed down interest and she learnt to teach the why and how and make it more scientific while remaining interesting. She did a lot of research on soaps and dyes and candle making, and ended up making specialised candle props for film makers. 'They want a candle to burn for a certain length of time, so I'd have to be able to supply candles that would do that.' Maureen worked on movies like *Women of the Sun*, *The Pirate Movie*, *Year of Living Dangerously*, *Muriel's Wedding* and others.

(Coincidentally, I too worked on *The Pirate Movie* as the National Parks Liaison Officer, because it was filmed in part of Port Campbell National Park, where I was stationed and training as a ranger. In fact, while we were on set my home became the production office during the day for renowned American director Ken Anninkin's staff. I was also present on *Women of the Sun*, also filmed near Port Campbell.)

Maureen and Dave's kids had always grown up using her 'homemade remedies and soaps and preparations for colds and were always into natural eating, like not peeling your carrots.'

For over twenty years Maureen had been exploring all sorts of herbal research. It was all around the house. 'We lived in an unusual "Cape Cod" house – very different. Our house always had a heap of bottles and jars and all sorts of stuff I'd be experimenting with. All the local kids used to come around – they thought I was a witch. I'd have them making soaps, cheese and other things. They'd also be painting rocks, carving soap – all gifts to take home. They loved it.'

An attack of breast cancer and then liver cancer, as well as deteriorating hips, made life extremely hard for Maureen. 'It taught me a lot about pain and survival and independence.'

When Maureen and Dave moved to the bush in 1988 she then 'got very heavy' into the herbal research of her life, even more so, studying energy aspects. She battled on through her illnesses with great dignity. Her orange VW Kombi with

SNAILS numberplate became a common sight around town, just a few miles from their bush home.

Maureen's work is not just a passing interest, it is her life passion and one she has made into a business. On the floor near where we are sitting in her crowded studio of bottles, jars, plants, special instruments and much more, is a number of 20-litre plastic drums, already sold to stores in the city. She supplies in large bulk to an ecology shop and also to a local co-op. She makes natural soaps, shampoos, conditioners, liquid cleaners, laundry and body washes, and other extracts that control hair lice, nappy rash creams and even mosquito repellents. There's no petroleum in her products; all are chemical free. She uses all sorts of natural bush plant ingredients and oils, and gets other raw materials from an ecologically aware pharmacy company owned by a chemist friend of hers, who now as a millionaire is able to be a world roamer, finding essentials oils, investigating sites where pollutants are and ensuring their cleansing.

Word of mouth has been good to Maureen's business too. She has also given lectures on her work and taught classes in all sorts of places, ranging from the Burnley Horticulture School to workshops at the local prison.

Some of the bottles in her studio contain essential oils from the Pacific, Middle East, England, Europe, South America (resins) and India (sandalwood). She says that Australian oil is the best in the world, particularly our sandalwood.

'Essential oils are like music. Loud music you hear the music, soft music you hear the instruments.' Maureen has a strong knowledge of world plants. Much of her work comes from very old books on the subjects of herbalism, plants and such, and as expected, she is a compulsive collector of plant books.

With Lee Wooster, a friend, Maureen co-authored a book titled *The Healing Botanical*. In the introduction they say: 'You're a jewel that holds the divine wisdom. This is a great gift, do not despair, shed the pain of the past and work with the flow of your destiny path. Spread your wings and soar to new heights in the understanding of your role on the earth plane.'

Maureen's studio contains a lifetime collection of plants, their extracts and her own collection of curiosities. 'All related to the journey, each thing is like a part of a jigsaw, but it slots into place. It may look a messy conglomeration but plants are what drives it all.'

Maureen commences making a bottle of oil for the bone disease in my arm. She wants me to try it. Now, I'm pretty sceptical but always willing to give anything a go at least once. No, it hasn't cured my bone disease, we never thought it would, but I must say it did cool and soothe some of the burning feeling often present in my arm. And I continue to use it. It is a smooth oil made up of balanced amounts of green oil, willow bark and leaf, plantain valerium, coffee bush, oakmoss, aloe vera and lavender.

Maureen continues with her interesting talk of sawdust from fruit trees fifty years old, being used to make brilliant colours. Parts of plants not affected by insects being used in the making of insect repellents, being mixed with frankincense, myrrh, sandalwood oils. Both cedar and Australian cypress, she says, make good insect repellents. Maureen says, 'The really rare is my thing, I like to still use them.

'We still haven't developed our full potential, I believe we are DNA encoded with information right back to the beginning of man.' Early civilisations used plants in healing, medicinal ways, so much of Maureen's knowledge potentially comes from centuries-old worlds.

Roses, lavender, salts, borax – all sorts of extracts go together for medicinal uses. Maureen showed me how three drops of an extract could give the powerful rose smell.

'Much of it evolves in my head when working with it. If you recognise your gift, you expand your work. I've been given a passion for plants and a need to know them intimately to use for people's pleasure and understanding to heal themselves. Did you know that yellow Hypericum flowers in oil turn it red? Or that the plant can relieve depression and aid sleep?

'All of this makes me boring to travel with. I always want to stop and check whether the red clover has been affected by roadworks fumes, etc. When we travel Dave talks of passing cars or whatever, I might talk of the St Johns Wort being in flower and they'll be sprayed soon. I work with many noxious weeds – they're lovely to work with.'

Maureen immediately goes off onto how nettles, for instance, are highly nutritious, are good blood cleaners and make great fabric. Beaten into a soft fibre, it can be bleached, and often was made into honeymoon sheets. She also adds enthusiastically that they also make beautiful paper.

So where did this interest come from for Maureen to follow it with such passion? Two women had a big influence on Maureen, both in different ways, but both inevitably helped her: her mother Cecilia Amelia (née Will) known as Ceilie and her grandmother Mary Josephine (née Carroll) known as Jo or Mary Jo or The Mater. As well as Maureen's memory of both, we should also thank her father Desmond, now 87, for his memories and for writing them out for me to add here.

MARY JOSEPHINE O'CONNELL
MAUREEN'S GRANDMOTHER

'She taught me to enjoy the smell of the earth, different smells of different stages of decay, she'd get quite ecstatic at that. She taught me about observing plants at different stages.

'She had an insatiable curiosity, she primed my curiosity to the various things,' Maureen recalls of her grandmother. 'We'd sit on the chookshed roof, for instance, and she'd show me things like how sun affected grapevine tendrils and make them grow, or she'd show me leaves that were shiny on one side and fluffy on the other. At the back fence there was pampas grass and she'd tell me how people ate the roots of plants, and we'd sit there eating pampas roots. There were fruit trees and vegetables, very sustainable land.

The garden was full of plants and not strictly a suburban type, as in those days the area was virtually bush. 'Texture and colour of plants was regarded as important,' says Maureen. 'She'd just show me things, and was always enthusiastic, never bored. And it was simplicity for small children to understand, never taught, she just had a way of doing it, like she was learning also. Insatiable.

'Shiny leaves to protect them from the sun. Some lemon trees had thorns and some types didn't. My grandmother was never impatient with me and my collecting stuff, which I've been doing for as long as I can remember. Always to feel, smell, see how things change. I learnt a bit about poisonous plants.

'Grandfather was always overcoming mechanical problems, always doing engineering stuff. Both grandparents were writers and Grandfather was also a great believer in recycling, he'd use a tin can to boil eggs in, and make tea in it as well. He believed it was a terrible waste to do otherwise. He was quite an eccentric gentleman.

'It was through Grandmother's marriage that I am a descendant of Daniel O'Connell, the Irish politician. She was a classic Irish mother; born in Dublin, she retained her broad cultured accent for her entire life and was appalled when a son acquired an Aussie ocker talk from school so had him have elocution lessons. She dominated the household, and had a very strong sense of place. She was versed in botany and Shakespeare. The family learnt German by speaking it at the meal table. She was a great card player. Her brother-in-law had been a head gardener in New Zealand at one stage.

'When my grandparents arrived in Australia they had a house built in Eglinton Street, Kew, which was then very rural. I can still remember as a tiny child the Chinese market gardener delivering stuff, and the iceman. Even bullock drays. The back verandah looked out over paddocks. They owned the first car in Kew, a 1919 Maxwell, and she didn't want it. Her son Desmond (Maureen's Dad) remembers how she used to sit in the back seat with a large triple bugle horn and constantly used it at every cross street to warn people, much to the family's embarrassment. One day coming down a steep hill a policeman had his hand up to stop, but with hardly any brakes, she continually blew the horn and yelled, "Keep going, he's only got a pushbike."

'Grandfather wanted to learn coach-building, but he was an

inventor and trouble shooter at Skipping Girl Brewery, working on things like stabilising yeast, which he devised the technique for.

The house was full of instruments, medieval lutes, a Stradivarius violin, piano, giant organ, trumpets, bagpipes and endless others. All the family played and sang.

'Grandmother was a beautiful piano player and had a beautiful voice. Grandfather was not a musician, though. They had four children including my father Desmond, now 87 and still going strong. He too is an amazing man. Even now he still invents stuff and works as a volunteer giving talks at Wyndana Drug Rehabilitation Centre. He and Dave my husband designed the chapel at Wyndana.

'My grandmother taught me how to make soap by rendering down fat. She also taught me things like how air moved over objects: she gave me a duck feather (off Dilly the duck), demonstrating how feathers moved in air. She'd pick others up and let them fall to show me. She always had something to say. She is my earliest memory up to about the age of six. I remember the smells of her kitchen, raspberry jams and the bread she made. Grandfather always had inventions happening in the kitchen. He made a bread slicer for her, and she was always angry as he'd be adjusting it.

'There was a fantastic pantry and us kids would climb in under the shelves and sit there. Grandfather always made things for us like a pedal train, golliwog and many movable wooden kangaroos that hopped, ducks and penguins that had moving flippers. He went on to set up the machinery for Ansell Rubber when they started in Australia.

'I also remember how he took us to see the mechanics of the

cable tram, just to show how it worked. He gave us the first experience of walking on metal gridding and ladders in the vinegar brewery. It was always adventures, not quite little girl type, on how things worked. His garage was full of all sorts of stuff like bench drills. He made canoes for the boys. Often Mary Jo would fall asleep in a canoe on the river.

'Mary Jo's sons were into photography and movie making, and she would be in the background giving directions – loudly.

'She was the person who introduced me to humour which was rather zany. She had a wacky sense of humour that could also be dark. She'd see it in all sorts of things. Incredibly inquisitive, and she was always a lady.

'It was a free home, not rigid. It was a whole family group – very powerful. Never a NO to something new. Warmth. A nesting thing. There was always a ton of books in the house.

'She was my first experience of death. I saw her in bed. It was hot. She still had her long red hair. It happened gently. She left such good memories.'

According to Maureen's father, Mary Jo died of pneumonia, and he remembers saying 'God bless you, Mum,' and she said, 'I hope he does.' He said she had style and was really something very special.

After she died and many years later Maureen moved in to live with her grandfather to care for him. Over the years people had worked at the place and caretakers gradually stripped off much of the stuff in the house. By the time Maureen moved in a lot of the wonderful stuff was gone. She helped for eighteenth months, then a lovely Dutch couple helped.

These memories of another time endure from a son and a granddaughter, memories of a lady of substance, one who left her mark for other generations.

'She made me aware of stuff that is very much in my life now,' says Maureen. 'I look at plants now in a way she taught me as a little girl. Now I'm passing it on to the next generation in my daughters and daughters-in-law.'

Something tells me Mary Jo would be very proud of her granddaughter's work.

CECILIA O'CONNELL
Maureen's Mother

'She allowed me to make my own choices and learn my own way. She was with us all the way no matter what. It was never "Don't do that", it was "Go have a go". She was a gentle teacher and always the most positive person looking at the positive side of things.'

Recently Maureen and her sister Annette were talking of their mother. Annette commented on how they could never be as amazing as their mother. Maureen agreed.

'Mother was a magnificent gardener. She loved the look. We had a bush garden. She loved music and had a clear voice. She sang all the time.'

Maureen's dad Desmond recalls that his wife was always 'singing and whistling in perfect pitch, turning everywhere we lived into comfortable nests, in a home that was being built around her. While bringing up the family, no glass or floorboards along the passage that connected all the rooms. Wind and rain were also part of our indoor lives. She was strong, sure and brave with a voice that made you feel good. Whatever she did she did well.'

So let's go back and find out more about her early life and to the home where 'wind and rain' came inside.

Cecilia's education stopped at grade three. Her mother had died giving birth to her sister, and so she had to look after her four sisters. Although part raised for a time by her grand-mother, her father remarried to a woman who didn't want his kids, so they were all put into Abbotsford Convent in Melbourne.

Her father couldn't afford to pay, so Cecilia had to look after the younger four sisters and also work at the convent that was now their home. Even then as a small child herself, 'she could see what other kids needed', as one of the nuns would remember many years later.

And so she stayed there with her sisters at the convent until she was ready to go out to work at Coles where she eventually became a manager. She later met and married Desmond O'Connell and started to raise a family. But Desmond had returned home from the war a restless man, and in 1948 he heard of a priest, a Father Pooley, who wanted to start a settle-ment in the bush and was looking for families. It was an experiment. The government was offering blocks of land and were wanting to experiment in decentralisation. It was to be a cooperative-run community, but it had to be a government approved plan.

The O'Connell family would be one of the first of seven families to join. Much of what would become known as Maryknoll community was virgin bush land near North Tynong, out of Melbourne towards Gippsland. There was a dairy farm included and the properties were five acres each, with a town centre. Each family gave some money to a credit union and brought what they could to the co-op. Desmond O'Connell had a joinery business making pre-fab schools.

The men went to the land first and started erecting three-room temporary houses for each of the seven families, until the permanent homes were built. One of the men was a master builder who taught the others. Former shop owners, labourers, even a chemist made up the families. Not all could cope.

The O'Connell, Corcoran, Tyler, Hunter, McSweeney, Murphy and Clancy families were the first to make up Maryknoll. Their accountant, Pat Clancy, would later become the Mayor of Moe.

And so Maureen, then 11, moved with the rest of the family to be with their father at Maryknoll in 1949, and she grew up there until 1955 when at 16 she left to go nursing.

'Maryknoll was a joy, a great place to live. There was enormous interaction between the families, and we kids would build huts down by the creek; it was a very free place to live. However, in those early years it was seen by others, including newspapers, as everything from a cult, to people who weren't allowed to leave there, to all sorts of weird things. None of it could have been further from the truth. Mum and Dad were very much involved in all aspects of it. Dad still lives there in the house they built. One of my brothers and his family also live there.'

Cecilia was always actively involved. She organised a group of women to help all other new women settle in. They'd get food, clean houses, look after kids, anything to help others. She organised the Maryknoll Fair every year and in early years many busloads would arrive from Melbourne to see what the place was all about.

She even managed to find time to have seven kids, including twins she had when she was over 40. Maureen was the eldest child and says, 'I can remember Mum in the kitchen still trying to help, and she was carrying and feeding the twins on each breast.' She was always the organiser. Maureen had a very strong connection to her mother as the eldest and Maureen believes 'her genetics dream was locked into mine when she died'.

Maureen's young sister designed the general store, and a community church, hall, fire brigade and post office were all built at Maryknoll. Cecilia was involved in organising the building of an elderly people's home there. Maureen says that 'today it is a large community, and quite up-market'.

Cecilia was a driven woman. She worked tirelessly for her family and her community, though she herself did find it hard to accept help from others. She became a big public speaker, and worked at an amazing range of community services. In 1981, she was made 'Woman of the Year' for her community service and numerous Girl Guides under her guidance earned Edinburgh Awards. The Cecilia O'Connell Travel Trust was set up to help Girl Guides travel the world.

She and her family were involved in postwar sponsoring of families from Holland. She and Desmond were active members of the *focolae* – a group of people who helped anyone in need throughout the world. They were also involved with a group who assisted street people. She was totally non-judgemental of people, whether they were drag queens or politicians.

Cecilia became District Commissioner for the Girl Guides, as well as regional camping adviser. Not a bad effort for a girl who left school in grade three. When she died the then Guiding Regional Commissioner said of Cecilia, 'She gave the purity of guiding to guiding.' Her beloved Guides crossed creeks on flying foxes to follow her to the graveside.

She got to know an amazing number and variety of people. She and Desmond travelled a lot overseas, and knew people all over the world. In 1981, when they knew she was dying, everyone rallied to make her days good. Musicians and choirs would come and perform for her, they had fireworks displays, dinners – everyone just wanted to thank her for all she'd done.

'Mum was always the gentle enthusiast and "out there",' says Maureen. 'It was always do and see something new with her. She never showed fear. She loved dancing as well as singing. She had a zany dry sense of humour, and was always the sergeant-major. An organiser right to the end.'

Even when she was dying of cancer at the age of 65, she organised everyone. Maureen was in charge of her body and did jobs like washing her. 'The boys were in the kitchen arguing about how they would carry her coffin and who would stand where to make it balanced,' she recalls. 'She heard them from her bed, called them all in and told them how it would be done, and sure enough it was carried perfectly balanced.

'She had a son-in-law make the coffin, and satin she had kept from Father Pooley was used to line the coffin. The builders asked if they could use the community truck to carry her coffin, which she was very happy about, and so it was all decorated with flowers and new paint.'

People came from various parts of the world to be at her funeral. From South Australia, Philippines, South America, France. A multi-millionaire friend, who had competed for her hand in marriage and lost, got them to delay the funeral until he could fly from Switzerland in his Lear jet, just so he could be there. Such was the impact this lady made on people.

Naturally, she was buried at Maryknoll.

The final words are from her husband Desmond:

> 'We watched the moon
> Race through the clouds
> Amongst our trees at night
> Simple wonders
> Close with God my love
> And now that's where she is,
> Always complete.'

And so there they are – three women of substance. All grandmothers, mothers and daughters who passed on to the next generation their own skills of life, all three an inspiration to all.

One of the Last Bohemians

BRUCE DAVIDSON

'I'VE HAD AN UNCONVENTIONAL LIFE – AND I STARTED EARLY.'

'We were always free and easy. Masters of our own destinies, we were the last of the bohemians. We really were.

'Once I take up a thing I give it my whole concentration. I make everything I need – house, furniture, vegie garden, booze, golf course. Why did I decide to build my own golf course? Sheer idiocy.'

'If he was reduced in size he'd look like a garden gnome' was how Bruce Davidson was first described to me. The person also added: 'He's a little champion, had an amazing life and a hell of a nice bloke.'

Well yes, he is small and could look like a gnome, and even has two pottery gnomes sitting in the window. One is playing a violin, which suits Bruce, as he is a violin player, and lover of classical music. Bruce also plays the mouth organ and the mandolin.

He is a potter, a good artist, and has had a lifetime of hard yakka. He's built fifteen houses with his own hands, made all his own furniture and at 71 still leads a very physical life. He has had a heart attack and quadruple bypass, but is currently carving his own 9-hole golf course out of the bush on a property that was thick with rubbish, gorse and hundreds of old car bodies.

He has made his own sly grog and even ended up in court for growing marijuana. He is a charming and sociable man who has many friends. The pub is as much his meeting place with friends as it is a place to drink.

While age might have tamed him a little, Bruce still has an aversion to authority, always has, but now he leads a quiet peaceful life in the bush.

Bruce was born in Auckland, New Zealand, in 1931, the son of a farming family at Pukekohe. At the age of 8 he moved with his family to an orchard north of Auckland. At 12 he was working a twelve-hour day on a stationary baling machine.

'The haybaling I did was the old-fashioned way, feeding wire into the bale, not using baling twine. It was hard yakka; I'd tie on average 1800 wires a day. I got paid 2/6d for every hundred bales, so I was averaging more a day than the average person who was on about 17/6d.

'I was sacked from school at 13 and a half for smoking.' At 14 he took over working the orchard, as his father was ill. 'We had about 5000 apple trees, 400 stone fruit trees, 100 oranges and 100 grapefruit. I worked from 5am until 10 at night. I'd start by finding and then milking the cows, feed the chooks and dogs. Then I had breakfast, then into the orchard all day spraying and moving heavy pipes and such, then home for milking again and chopping the wood. After tea I'd go into the shed to make packing cases for the fruit. I did that six-and-a-half days a week, with just Saturday afternoon off.

'I'd always been interested in magic, and Dad taught me tricks when I was about six or seven. I learnt more over the years, and then for two years in Auckland I worked professionally as a magician. I had a dual act with a mate who was a singer. We did a heap of shows, for the Masons (1500 people), 300–400 at private functions – anybody that was having a big do. I ended up a part of the inner circle of magicians.'

Music has always been a part of Bruce's life. 'I started to learn the mouth organ at four, then the mandolin at seven and the fiddle at nine. I had lessons and could read music by the time I was 7. I last played in a local Irish band some twenty years ago.

'At school I was into all sports, everything. Athletics. I was good at sports due to illness. I had blood noses for years. My big brother was built strong. I was skinny. I became a fanatic to build myself up and be strong like my brother. I did weightlifting, and I was always doing pull-ups: even when I walked through a door, I'd pull myself up by the fingers until I reached the top of the door. I was a total fanatic at building my body. I was also trained at judo.

'I went to the city at 16 and my first job was filling quilts with feathers. Then I was a bottle stacker in a soft drink factory. Later I worked in a mill and did machine pressing of socks. I was always looking for something, I did everything.

'When I went to sea as an ordinary seaman, there was nothing to pinch. At 19, I was in the seamen's union and working on the *Tuhoe*, a 130 foot scow, as an ordinary seaman. She had two 240hp diesel engines and we traded up and down the coast. Drums of petrol on the deck, we'd take wheat down the coast and bring 150 ton of butter on the return trip. I worked on her for a year, then on to *Tainui*, a new ship, and worked there for nearly a year. Then about 1951, there was the biggest strike ever in New Zealand, and we were on strike for four months.

'I became a light delivery truck driver, and was doing some fiddling on the side. Then I worked in dispatch, later became an insurance salesman, then sold typewriter ribbons, worked in a clothing factory, sold cricket bats and worked in a sports store. Then I was at an ice cream factory and had a good sideline selling Eskimo pies. I even used to slap two Eskimo pies into the hands of the policeman on point duty in the main street of Auckland as I went by in the truck. I had a great racket – say I had an order for 12 dozen Eskimo Pies, I'd give them 24 dozen: I'd pocket the money for the extra six dozen and they'd get the other six free. It was a great racket. I did everything.'

'They wanted me to do National Service but I refused. The police told me I'd have to, and I just said no, I'm not going to do it. And I didn't.

'I came to Australia in 1956, and was selling books door-to-door. I also sold advertising. Then I moved to Tasmania as manager, training sellers on how to sell books. Then I sold pine plantations.

'I returned to Melbourne, and was spending weekends learning about hypnotherapy. I had first started to read about it when I was 16 and I've always had an interest in eastern religion, Chinese history and such. I'm still very interested in it.

'At 17, I saw an ad in the paper looking for a young person interested in eastern religion. I met a yogi from a monastery.

He was the first to hypnotise me. I spent a lot of time learning from books. With two other blokes we studied hypnotherapy, and I went to both Melbourne and Sydney hypnotherapists to learn from others, including Ainsley Meares, the well-known psychiatrist.

'At the time *Encyclopaedia Britannica* had coupons, and if you sent them in they'd send you all the data you wanted on the subject. There wasn't a lot available on hypnotherapy at that time, but I bought every book I could about it, and ended up practising full time, doing it for two or three years – doing things like helping people to give up smoking, biting nails, nervous disorders, picking skin and warts and even stopping bed-wetting.'

It was all just another small part in the amazing life of Bruce Davidson.

'Then one day someone said to me "come see the mud houses" and I absolutely loved it and soon ended up living at Dunmoochin and stayed from 1961 to 1972.'

Dunmoochin became a famous artist colony, thirteen homes on 157 acres of bush at the Cottlesbridge–Eltham–Hurstbridge area near Melbourne. It was home to artists such as Clifton Pugh, where the rules were no dogs, no cats, no gardens, and no fences except the boundary. It was there he grew to know all sorts of people who came and went. People like Alvin Toffler, author of *Future Shock:* 'He stayed for a party en route to Indonesia to write a book. We all got pissed by 2am and at 5am I was supposed to take him for a tour of the property, but he didn't make it.'

Bruce's memories of others include artist John Percival – 'a talented painter but difficult.' Artist Fred Williams – 'Strange, when we met a few times he'd always be in a suit and I'd just be in shorts and nothing else, covered in mud or clay.' Artist John Olsen – 'Affected in a benign way. He taught me how to make Spanish paella.'

Many others came to visit and to party at Dunmoochin – like Labor federal and state politicians Clyde Holding, who 'came up occasionally', and Jim Cairns, 'a lovely man'. Governor-General Lord De L'Isle was 'a nice chap'.

Of course, Bruce became a long-time friend of Clifton Pugh. 'I liked Cliff very much. We had our differences, absolutely! I know in one argument I walked away and gave him a home I'd built. I loved our life down there, it was free and easy and we were all masters of our own destinies. They were wonderful people. Free bohemians.'

Bruce spend a great deal of time in his own studio making pottery, and excelled. He continued his interest in building, and did a lot of work on all the homes at Dunmoochin. 'I worked a lot making mud bricks. I did what I wanted to, basically.'

He also did a lot of house wrecking. One job included taking nine 7-ton-truckloads of timber and stuff from the Mitcham Tile Works. On other jobs he said he did a lot of 'poozling' – or, as he describes it, 'saving stuff from destruction without paying for it'.

'We started to have art shows and all sorts of stuff at the place and soon up to 700 people would turn up at weekends to see the colony. People would buy a pottery mug, we'd give free beer away, they'd get pissed and then buy more stuff, so finally the police closed the shows down after three years, because by the time people left to drive home they'd be pissed. I later started my own pottery shows and did it for seven years.'

His pottery work has sold far and wide. 'Once I made some large platters and Fred Williams decorated them and they ended up in the National Gallery in Canberra. They are still there.'

As for marriage and kids, Bruce says he has had several partners. 'I never let them down. I never married, but I had three partners over a twenty-five-year period.'

'In 1972 I built the first mud brick house at Golden Point on 20 acres and began to teach others in the district how to as well. And I built a second shack on 7 acres. I split up from my partner in 1975 so I moved back to Dunmoochin for a year.

For a small man, Bruce Davidson has led a physically demanding life and one home he constructed shows his determination to build. A home near where he now lives in central Victoria bears testimony to his strength, endurance and determination. The local paper did a two-page feature story on it, describing it as a local landmark. *Home Beautiful* magazine, in a four-page colour feature, described it as the 'ultimate hideaway' and judged the home as one of the finalists, but not overall winner, in the 1990 Home of the Year competition.

When Bruce first took over the block he built a one-room shanty which took him 'about two weeks and 40 bucks to build'. 'When I came here I was the only person in the whole valley. I came here for peace and quiet, to play my classical music and enjoy the solitude of the bush.'

He then set about building his dream home in February 1979, called Pax (which means 'peace' in Latin). It took ten years of hard yakka for Bruce to build the home. The site was blasted out of the side of a hill. He moved 1000 tonnes of bush stone and slate to build walls of the bottom floor of the home, terrace and stone garden walls a metre high that line the driveway 60 metres below. One of the slate slabs in the floor weighed a tonne and a half.

'All the stone was carted from river beds and quarries in an old Chev with no doors, no windows, no lights and practically nothing else,' says Bruce with a laugh. 'I moved 800 tonnes just for the retaining walls in the garden which were 180 feet long and 13 feet high, and there was 48 tonnes of slate in the house.'

Bruce was no stranger to building houses. He built three Dunmoochins in the Castlemaine area, one at Yarrambat, and worked on many others. He also helped enlarge a studio for artist Albert Tucker at Hurstbridge. From memory he thinks he's built fifteen in all, and helped many other people get started on their own mud-brick homes.

The second floor was added in beautifully warm old Oregon and pine timbers along with some amazing stained glass windows. Pax comprised two bedrooms, open kitchen, living room, billiard room and cellar. To save space inside, the stairway to the second storey folded up into the ceiling when not in use.

When he was quoted $18,000 to add electricity, he solved the problem by devising his own self-sufficient home. Hot water came from a custom-made steel fireplace and in summer the water was heated with solar panels. More solar panels also kept electricity pumping for the stereo and television. The fridge was run by gas.

Beautifully made brass gas lamps that he made kept it lit at night. Water was stored in tanks above and below the house. Varied artworks adorned the walls and statues the garden. It truly was one man's hard yakka and creative mind that built a much-talked-of house, in a time when things like stone and solar houses were uncommon, unlike today.

Today people still talk about the round steel fireplace Bruce made from an old 2-metre-tall hot water storage cylinder, an old-looking boiler type he cut holes into for the fireplace, oven and drying box, with some ornamental doors a blacksmith friend made for him. The bottom section was used as a drying box or warming oven, and above it the firebox produced boiling water via a hot water coil.

Above the main firebox was the main oven, with a flue going upstairs that heated the upstairs billiard room and was then diverted to go out to the smokehouse on a skillion roof. Another narrow stone cavity with inlets and outlets in the wall allowed it to also heat another room at the rear. Three logs used to take thirty hours to burn, so efficient was his design.

People came from near and far to see Bruce's creation. He taught many people the art of building from mud, and helped others in their creative efforts. He was one of the first in the district to build from slate, which abounds from the goldfields days.

But then he sold the home. 'Then I lost money on investments in China. I was going to settle in Tasmania and at one stage was going to live on Flinders Island in Bass Strait. I was negotiating to buy a big barge but I missed out on what would have made a great home. I was going to alter it and build something special. The bloke who owned the barge went and sold it.'

In 1988 Bruce suffered a heart attack and had a quadruple bypass. 'I returned to the valley here and ended up building this smaller place on this block almost across the road from the original big place I built. I've been here now for six years.

'I just couldn't stand to see this property abandoned and the land destroyed. I've worked every day for five years trying to improve it. I spent 3800 hours just cleaning the place up, removing acres of wild gorse and lots of old car bodies scattered through the bushland.'

It's hard to imagine now, because he has built a scenic and inspiring valley. 'I've got a ride-on mower with a seven foot cutter and the valley is set with sprinklers fed from the dam, but the drought has ruined me. I'm getting tired and a bit pissed off. I've spent a heap of money doing it all. As for my golf interest, years ago I saw great golfers like Sam Sneed, Thompson and Nagle play. I play about two games a year now. I took it up when I was sick, to try and help me breathe.

'Pissed! I first got pissed at 13 and I'm still at it.'

Years ago Bruce was known as the local moonshiner. He started selling rum for a friend. He sold it everywhere, to various parts of Australia. 'I was buying it for myself but then started to sell it and I took over from a friend. He became a mine manager in Western Australia. Back home in New Zealand on the south island everyone made their own grog. Hokonui Moonshine Rye on the south island has been famous for a hundred years plus, I don't know what all the fuss is here. I learnt how to make it by reading books, mainly using molasses, eleven days to ferment and three days to distil. When I was at it I used to sell ten flagons a week to one pub alone.'

Bruce used to make not only beer, but rum, whisky and

more. But having an illegal still was asking for trouble. I tasted some of the last of the moonshine he ever made. He knows how to brew.

'For a long time I used to supply pubs who couldn't get enough of it, and if you are ever in Western Australia ask the fishing fleet at Port Hedland about my rum. I got them pissed for a fortnight once,' he laughs.

He also likes the taste of other brewers' work. 'I was pissed at the Guildford pub one night and about 2am I decided to go home, and they all said, "No, you can't drive home." "It's okay," I said. "There'll be no one around and I'll just sneak up the track." So I'm doing 40kph and sure enough the police pull me up. "What'd ya pull me up for? I wasn't speeding," I said. "No, sir, you weren't, but you are on the wrong side of the road." "I must be pissed," I said. I lost my licence. I've lost it three times all told.'

Always prepared to 'push the envelope' somewhat, it has sometimes caught up with him. Getting into trouble has been something Bruce has accepted as part of his life. 'I've always reacted to authority, I believed we shouldn't be directed from birth to the grave by self-seeking politicians.'

I'd heard of one locally famous incident and wasn't sure if I should broach the subject, but as Bruce is very open, he soon told me the story.

'I'd just come out of hospital. I was still sick. I walked down through the bush, when suddenly about six blokes in forestry uniforms and six Police SOG (Special Operations Group – 'people call them "Sons of God", 'cause they think they are) officers came at me. They'd staked me out for 10 days and had all been booked in at the local pub and spent up big. They surrounded me and I was arrested and later on the ABC news that night.

'They didn't catch a bunch of drug dealers, but they played it up as a major 2.4 kilogram, $320,000 drug haul. All they caught was one sick 58-year-old man with his own "pot" plants – 140 of them.

'Anyway at court, I represented myself, I did my homework, I'm no idiot. Finally the judge said, "I find the charges proven. For your age, I can't understand why you did this. You're a remarkable man but I will not convict you or fine you." And that was it.

'Part of my defence was that as I can't smoke, I only made pot cookies. We reckon the stake-out cost the police force about $20,000. And I can tell you I have since given the recipe to a police officer.'

Life now is quieter for Bruce. He lives with his lovely seven-year-old kelpie dog Gilly, a wonderfully intelligent and friendly dog. Great for a man who lives quietly in the Australian bush growing his vegetables, building his golf course and listening to his large collection of the classics. 'I've been reading 500 pages a week minimum, always, since I was a kid. I still have five sets of encyclopaedias. I'm addicted to ancient history, I read anything I can get, it's a huge interest to me. I've always respected people who taught me something.'

And so, for a man who has had his own slice of life, how does he describe it all now? 'I've had the most wonderful life, enjoyed every minute of it. I always felt free to do what I wanted in life, so long as I didn't hurt anyone.'

Birdman of Horseshoe Lagoon

MICK 'GRUMPY' BETSON

'A GOOD-HEARTED OLD FELLOW. HE WAS JUST A BUSHIE,
A COUNTRY BUMPKIN, A JACK-OF-ALL-TRADES.'

I was staying in Moama, New South Wales, at Misty Gums Cottages that back onto and overlook the Horseshoe Lagoon. It was the middle of November 2002 and it was one of the worst droughts for years across Australia. It had even reached the Murray River, which was lower than usual and the lagoon I was told was some eight feet lower than normal.

It was 6am and I decided to go for a walk along the banks of the Murray and around the lagoon that came off the main river. I had nearly completed the walk when I came across a small plaque in a redgum post near the roadway.

It's only a small plaque and now starting to show the effects of weather, but it says a little of the man known as Grumpy. People probably stop and read it and move on and think 'that's nice'. But for me it was more. I wanted to know who Grumpy was.

Immediately I knew he must have been an interesting man, and I wanted to know more. In my mind I nicknamed him the Birdman of Horseshoe Lagoon. It has a great ring to it, and I think he probably would have approved.

Wild ducks and other birds that are prevalent around Horseshoe Lagoon can thank the late Mick 'Grumpy' Betson. He started feeding birds at the lagoon with scraps in the late 1970s.
His actions attracted more and more birds and he even installed what was known as 'Jacaranda Lodge', a floating maternity hospital for birds.
As the birds still come and feed and give pleasure to locals and visitors alike, it will be Grumpy's gentle kindness that will be carried on their wings forever.
In the Memory of 'Grumpy'
Michael Ernest Lawrence Betson

The owner of the place I was staying didn't know who Grumpy Betson was. I had to head for home, but was determined I'd find out more. Eventually, I spoke by phone to his widow and his daughter, and knew I needed to return to Moama.

No one remembers exactly when Mick first started work at the lagoon but it was about fifteen or more years before he finally died in 1983. If it wasn't for the small plaque there, probably no one would remember in time. But he deserves to be remembered.

Alice Betson is now 83 years of age, and a bit frail. Her health hasn't been the best but she invited me into her unit in the centre of town. She was more than happy to remember and pass on details to me. She said she gets a bit confused with dates and that her daughter, just out of town, would help more.

'The kids idolised him, but he used to say, "I'm just a grumpy old bugger." Yet he was nothing like that. He was a real country person, always mad about the river and boats. He made his own little boat. It was used in the TV mini-series *All the Rivers Run*. And he was always mad on animals. His real name was Ernest but he was nicknamed Mick. All the kids just called him 'Grumpy' and many people would not have even known his real name.'

Mick was born and bred in the bush. He and Alice met and were married in 1937 and had two girls and a boy. His father worked all his life on the railways as a ganger, and Mick was working on a bridge gang for the railways waiting for a call to join the war. He spent the war years in the RAAF, and served in the New Guinea islands. His daughter Hellen told me later that her father never spoke of the war, and that he still had shrapnel in his back when he died. He was repatriated home from Moratai to Heidelberg Hospital to convalesce and was there a long time. He would never fully recover.

Mrs Betson continued. 'From then on he couldn't always work full time due to his health, but he always tried to do a decent day's work, which he believed in. He wasn't lazy. He was a jack-of-all-trades, and very popular. People said he was one of the best fencers around, and he did it for a long time when he could. He picked up a lot of handyman jobs, fencing and mustering. People would just wait for him when he was feeling okay. Many of the farmers liked his work. Numerous times we camped as caretakers for farmers, to look after their homes and properties.'

His daughter Hellen also remembers he worked on the river

in the forties, when they floated logs down the river behind barges.

In 1972, the Betsons bought a little milk-bar. 'People would come knocking on the door at all hours saying their baby had run out of milk,' so after three years they sold it as it was too much for Mrs Betson.

Mick ended up a TPI pensioner due to his war service. One day he said to his wife 'the lagoon needs a bit of beautifying'.

'I think he decided to do it to take his mind off himself, he'd just been going from one thing to another.'

Hellen and her husband Alan, a champion shearer, remember the lagoon when they were growing up as kids. It was never called Horsehoe Lagoon then, but always known as 'The Dock' as there was the wharf for the paddleboats, and a swimming hole. The dock is gone now except for a few rotting timbers, and a new wharf has been built a bit further along at the entrance to the lagoon.

'We lived two streets from the lagoon,' says Mrs Betson. 'Mick just started to clean it up, removing rubbish and stuff. He didn't ask the council permission, he just did it.'

He planted different trees, and louts would pull them up as fast as Mick planted them. The lagoon is next to a caravan park and tourists didn't worry about the area much. 'He also planted climbing geraniums. Then waterlilies, but they were swiped. He made redgum seats. He scrounged all sorts of stuff. Many of the wealthy farmers started to give him more and more waterlilies from their ornamental lakes. He just continued on. Once a young girl let her horse eat all his plants.'

In those days it was not developed like it is today and Mick had his challenges. Tourist people at the caravan park would come down with their shotguns to shoot ducks.

'Mick ended up in many arguments with people, particularly the foreigners who were very nasty. Many nights he'd go down there, and many nights I'd talk him out of it – I'd say if they are silly enough and cruel enough, let them. He'd lie there in bed listening and complain to me for the next week about it. We had quite a few arguments about it all. But, really doing the work there at the lagoon, I think it saved his life.

'We were extremely cross with the local shire council who were uninterested and wouldn't even lend Mick a hose. They didn't want to know about it. So he carted his own hose from the house down each time and he'd drag that heavy hose around to water plants. The council were very much against it all, and he had numerous confrontations. They blamed him for the ducks crossing the road saying it might cause an accident. They did nothing at the lagoon. They didn't see the joy it brought to an old man and to the many people who went there to feed the birds.'

Mick just persevered year after year. He had introduced a couple of his own muscovey ducks to the lagoon in an attempt to attract wild ducks, and gradually it worked. More and more birds arrived and called the lagoon home. In the end Mick had the whole town supplying food for 'his' ducks. Greengrocers would supply green feed. Bakers supplied stale bread, farmers supplied oat and wheat seconds. He scrounged whatever he could. Much of it also came from what he bought out of his own pocket. And some of it came from the Betson garden – apples, apricots, grapes.

He loaded his trailer. 'Every morning you could put your

clock on it, Mick would head off until lunchtime. Then he'd come home for lunch and all through lunch he'd say, I must do this and have to do that – all for the lagoon. He did a lot of talking.

'He liked to meet strangers down there and talk. He always spent time with kids, and loved to give them food to feed the ducks. There were several swans there, many black ducks, white ducks, ibis, all sorts. Oh, he was a character, he saved a lot of birds I'd say.

'He'd be furious to see what they've done now, after all those years of them neglecting it and complaining. He'd see red.'

Mick even scrounged enough timber to build a floating duck hospital. 'They were demolishing either an old bank or hotel, I can't remember, but anyway he scrounged enough timber from them to build his floating hospital. It was a sort of boat with boxes in it, so any injured bird could recover there, or they could raise their babies in there also. Even the *Bendigo Advertiser* sent a reporter up to Moama to write a story on Mick.

Mick had two staunch supporters who did some fighting for him. Alex Witney, the local mailman, wrote to the *Riverina Herald*, and Merv Buckley, who worked on the council, 'used his tongue'. 'They were both great supporters and did a lot to help.'

I asked Mrs Betson if she also worked at the lagoon. 'Oh no, I had plenty of work at home. My days were always busy with family and I always had a nice garden. The lagoon was his work and interest. He spent his life there and it extended his life. He was just rapt in it.'

Hellen remembers her father as a 'good-hearted old fellow'.

His son-in-law Alan says he was a great father-in-law who loved his fishing and had a great love for the river.

Mick died on 15 March 1983. He was 64 years old. His heart and lungs finally gave in.

His wife Alice remembers him fondly. 'He was just a bushie, a country bumpkin. He just loved the country social mixture of neighbours, and he'd talk on any subject. He was a jack-of-all-trades.'

The small plaque at the lagoon was not one the shire decided to install. It came about because of the love of Mick's grand-daughters, Dianne and Susan, who thought of it and pushed for it to be done. They spoke to Robert Caldwell on the Murray Shire Council, and the family were grateful for his interest. He immediately organised it and within three months it was installed.

The importance of Mick Betson's work is more than just his interest in the lagoon, though it did give him purpose, peace and a sense of achievement. It is bigger than that, though. He set an example for all small communities – to participate, to persevere, not give in to petty bureaucracy, to stand by one's own ideals and dreams and reach a goal. And to pass on to the next generation the joys one can find in simple pleasures like feeding ducks on a lagoon.

A few years ago the council started work on the area and spent many thousands of dollars creating a bridge and board-walk that went through the area, creating walking paths and seating, for tourists to enjoy. A friend of the family said Mick would be seeing red if he was alive today, to see they finally have done something there and yet for years neglected it and tried to dissuade him from his efforts. But it just goes to show that Mick had foresight and knew a good spot worth preserving.

The owner of the Misty Gum Cottages that overlook the lagoon told me they have many people stay there and enjoy the lagoon. Some elderly people in particular sit with binoculars to watch the birds, and one man said he counted over 160 species around the area.

I can attest to the numerous birds there, even in the worst drought, and although I didn't see 160 species I enjoyed many ducks, a family of ibis and dozens of smaller birds like blue wrens, finches and others. A pair of black ducks even came across the grass to the window of the cottage I stayed in, looking for a feed. I happily obliged, knowing Mick would have approved.

Thanks, Mick – your legacy will continue. You really were the Birdman of Horseshoe Lagoon.

'John'

TIME WITH A FREE SPIRIT
'IT'S A GOOD WAY TO WATCH THE WORLD GO BY.'

Earlier in this book I told you about an old man, Mr McKinnon the swagman, not knowing when I included his story that before I finished the book I would be writing of a similar man who came into my life, this one much younger – John. (He goes by the name of his two Christian names reversed, and I will not use his family surname here out of respect for his wishes and the family's privacy.)

I was travelling south from Echuca. About 20 kilometres south I saw him on my side of the road walking towards me. He was heavily laden and he plodded along head down, a large hat probably keeping flies off his face (rather than the sun, as it hadn't emerged from the clouds as yet). I drove past him, and saw he was a relatively young man. I drove a bit further thinking of the sight I'd just seen but knew I had to go back.

I did a u-turn and retraced my path driving past him again and then when far enough down the road, did a u-turn and parked off road and waited for him to come along.

'Like a drink, mate?' I said, holding up a bottle of cold water. He stopped. 'I've got plenty of water, thanks,' he replied, motioning to one of the large potato bags he was carrying.

I introduced myself and we shook hands. I explained about the book and as he sat back against his bags, I sat in the thick pile of dried bark that surrounded the tree. Tiny ants soon emerged to crawl across my jeans to check me out. It didn't matter, I sensed an interesting story. Trucks and cars roared past at great speed, making it hard to hear him speak at times. A quiet, softly spoken man. He seemed relaxed, if not perhaps a little bit wary at first. Couldn't blame him for that.

He said his name was John. 'Just John will do.' I wrote it down, hoping that as I gained his confidence I might get more, but it was up to him. And so we began what ended up being about an hour-and-a-half of half interview and half chatting.

John is a walker, a road traveller, a modern-day swagman, a scavenger, a loner. He is all that and more but for himself he is just content. All that we would call him doesn't mean much to him. 'They're all just labels,' he says. 'Labels just are a vision in other people's eyes, it doesn't really say who you are.'

I had to agree, society does tend to categorise each other into good and bad. 'I'm just me,' he reinforces quietly.

When I asked how long he'd been a traveller, he replied, 'Over 25 years'. I was shocked. He didn't look an old man by any stretch of the imagination. I learnt that he was 48 and had first hit the road at just 'twenty-two or three' years of age. So young for a man to decide to call it quits from society. I sensed there must have been some traumatic reason, but only gently questioned him in a roundabout way as to how it all happened as I didn't want to put any undue pressure on him.

I wanted to take him back to his early days but really felt that may have been intruding, so was careful what I asked. But he responded without too much hesitation. Only on a couple of occasions when he looked off into the distance or down I felt he needed time to decide how to answer. His sharp clear blue eyes were penetrating but not threatening. I saw a deep thinker. They say the eyes are the windows to the soul.

John has amazing clear blue eyes. 'You're not the first to comment about that,' he said. By now we had settled more and our conversation became more free and relaxed. The cars and trucks still rushed by. John continued to lie back on his belongings against the tree. Legs outstretched. He seemed to be enjoying the yarn.

'I was born at Minyip in Victoria. My father was a painter and tiler. I moved to Melbourne to start work with the Commonwealth Bank and stayed there for four years. I worked as a bank teller and a bit of this and that in the head office. It was good. I fitted in alright with people and I was content amongst crowds but I was always a bit on the fringe, I guess.

'I got out before the computers took over. I prefer to do things at my own pace. I didn't really make the decision to do all this, I just didn't want to tie myself down. I wanted to do a bit of hitching for three months and so ended up going up through to Katherine, in Northern Territory, across to Wyndham in Western Australia, down to Perth and back across to Adelaide. I like walking. No hurry. I've just kept walking. Over the years I've done odd jobs here and there fruit picking and log-burning and other stuff, but now I mainly depend on the road.'

I asked him to explain more about depending on the road.

'Just living on what I find. I picked up three dollars and two socks so far today.' John wasn't worried about being seen as a scavenger, as he called it.

He survived on his own, burdened no one and lived by his own unspoken rules, although he says he just lives day by day and never has a routine. 'I might make plans but I find things often change. I'd plan to go a certain route, but I see a road go off that I might decide to follow instead.'

When talking with John you soon learn that his landmarks aren't like ours. We'd say we're going to Echuca from Bendigo, but John talks by roads. He mentions the Hume, the Goulburn Valley, the New England, the Pacific Highway.

I had to push a bit more to learn more of his routes, so he threw in some names of towns. I was trying to learn more of where he travelled. 'I have a bit of a route each year, but now I'm finding I take in other roads as well. Generally I travel down as far as Seymour, to the junction about five miles out, then head up the Hume Highway as far as Bargo, Sydney, then end up north, and towns I always see are Goulburn, Lismore, Moree, Tenterfield, Gravesend, and back down and then across via Hay, Deniliquin to Mildura. After Echuca I'm headed towards Shepparton, then down to Seymour then back up north. But I always travel on and off the main roads now.'

It is obvious there's a reason for John to take many of the busier roads. People throw stuff out their vehicles. It is how John survives. 'I'm amazed what they throw out. The Newell Highway is the best for money. On the Hume Highway in

Victoria I make two or three dollars a day picking up coins on the side of the road as I walk. Some days I might find a lot of small coins, you know, 5 and 10 cent pieces; other days I might just find one or two larger coins. It depends on the road.'

I asked John how he thought people lost money. 'I've stopped asking myself that question a long time ago,' he replies with a smile. 'About two years ago I found $20 in one day. At one spot there was about 10 dollars' worth of coins scattered, and further on at some roadworks I found about six dollars. I was walking around shoving it all into a sock. You'd never expect to find money on bridges, would you. People wouldn't park there, but I've even found money on bridges.'

I asked if there were days when he found nothing, and he nodded yes, but it wasn't only money he looked for. 'I mainly live off the road now. I get my tucker, clothes, footwear, reading material. All stuff people throw out the car window. Might be half a roll to eat or some fruit. Occasionally people stop and give me something. Yesterday a lady in Rochester gave me two muffins and some homemade lemonade as I passed through, but I never hang around. I always get out of towns. I scrounge in town but town rubbish bins are now made "less user-friendly to scavenging",' he says with a laugh. 'But you can always find food in most towns. My aim is always to get out of town before night. And I always camp before I get into a town, that way I have all the next day to pass through.'

This collecting off the roadside amazed me, and John agreed. 'It still stuns me what I find.' But I was interested about what he obtained, and soon learnt just about everything the man has is what he's found. He points to his running shoes. They are different colours and brands but both fit pretty well.

'For years I always wore thongs. I'd find them all the time and carried a few pairs, all different. I might have three right foot ones before I found a left one. Now, though, I prefer these rubber shoes, not the hard ones. I go through about three or four pairs of shoes a year. It's strange, I might find a shoe, and then walk on and another mile or so I find the other one. The first thing I do is check the size.

'I always find piles of socks, and I pick up every one. I usually hang them off the back of my bag and let them air out for a while. I've already found two today.'

Even John's potato bags he found, making one into a haversack and another to carry. 'You don't find them much any more, though,' he says wistfully. 'Most of my bags last about three or four months. I have a clean-out about every six to twelve months, and start again.' Everything he owned was in the couple of bags. He had a few clothes, one blanket, a sleeping bag, some clear plastic sheeting to keep the rain off when required, some books and magazines. 'I always like to read,' he said. (I gave him a copy of *Beaut Utes 4*, my latest book, which he was very happy to get – reading truly was a big thing for him. Helped to pass the time away no doubt.)

'That's the advantage of walking. You get to read whatever you find. I like to read fantasy and science fiction, though.'

John does have regular people he sees. He is well known in some areas, and he even has a few people who give him shelter and odd jobs. 'There's three folk who invite me to call in whenever I pass.

'One old lady near Drake in Queensland has 50 acres and I usually stay there for three weeks, to help carry and move stuff for her. She's a bit unsteady on her feet. I dig holes or do any heavy work for her. She might even be dead by the time I get there this time. She is pretty old.'

I asked John what did his life on the road mean to him and how much longer will he do it.

'I'm content. That's the only word I can think of. I got no real hassles. I just have more freedom. I don't know about the future, I just live each day. I suppose I will have to stop it one day – if I last that long.'

I asked about his health. 'Last time I went to the doctor was when I was about 18 when I had a medical examination to join the bank.'

What was the best and worst about being on the road, I asked. 'Content. Just that I'm content I guess.'

And the worst thing about being on the road? He had to think. 'I don't really find anything, I'm a bit too casual I guess, nothing worries me much. Sometimes I might have to tighten my belt a bit – I'm not going to put on weight,' he says with a quiet laugh.

'I'm always alert for food,' he says. I'm sure John will never be overweight eating leftover scraps he finds on the side of the road. But does he ever buy food? 'Sometimes if I have a bit of money I might. Usually spaghetti or baked beans, or if I want something better I might get a stew or a hot pie.

'The longest I'd go without any food at all would be about three or four days, but usually I find something to keep me going. Sometimes it might be up to a fortnight without very much or I'll be real short. I feel empty then, but I never get hunger pains. At those times I usually drink a lot more water.'

I was surprised to learn that John rarely carries his own water. I thought that with the drought so bad he'd certainly need it, but it didn't seem too big a deal for him. 'There's usually plenty of dams or creeks around. On my routes I generally know where there's water. At the moment I'm carrying some, though.

'I also carry a transistor radio, and listen to it when I've got batteries. But I'm okay so long as I've got something to read.'

When John told me he carried a transistor radio, I wondered what he thought of when he heard the news of the world.

'Life – I don't understand half of it. I just take each day as it comes. Something always changes.' I knew he just wanted not to be a part of it, and do his own thing.

I wanted to know about the dangers or problems of life on the road. 'Occasionally you might get someone throw something at you and yell something out, but they are usually going that fast you can't hear them anyway; that's happened a couple of times. The only other thing in twenty-five years on the road is I've had my gear stolen twice. Two kids on Cowra took off with my bag when I was going to the toilet, and then at Swansea at a park area someone stole my gear. But other than that, no real problems.

'I did have one accident. I was sitting under a big gumtree reading, and the next thing I know I'm flat on my stomach. A big branch from high up broke off and hit me. I was laid up unable to walk. I had some tucker and luckily I'd seen a big puddle of water right near me. I think I had bruising all around here.' He motioned to his back and side. Sounded as if his lungs and ribs would have been hit hard. Possibly cracked ribs. He didn't go to a doctor.

'I had to lie there for four days to feel up to walking again, even though it was gingerly. It really knocked me.'

One aspect of bush life John has never liked. Snakes.

'This last trip from Deniliquin to Hay there were a lot of snakes. On the road, they'd just pop up and they'd go one way, and I'd go the other. Never had any in my camps, always just on the road or on the side of it. I never liked them.'

So what sort of camp does John make each night at the end of the long day of walking?

'I always just get off the road and try and put a bush between me and the road, and not be too obvious. If I find a bridge I always take advantage of it, getting underneath. I very rarely have a fire, even in winter, not worth it. Just as easy to roll out the sleeping bag and just get in. Always have to get warm before I stop, though. If your feet are cold when you get into bed you never get them warm, but if you walk it's okay. In the morning it takes about an hour to get warm and get the blood flowing.'

So if he doesn't light fires, does he ever cook? 'No, I always eat everything cold.' What about boiling a billy for a cup of tea? 'No, I just drink water or soft drink.'

This haphazard inconsistent diet may have already taken some toll on John. Whilst he is a lean but fit-looking bloke, he has lost some of his teeth, but it doesn't seem to worry him.

The flies were pretty consistent as I interviewed John, so I asked if they or mosquitoes worry him, but already guessed you just have to get used to them. I also asked about the sun, noticing his tanned arms were very freckled. 'I might some-times have some suncream but I'm very frugal with it, use it mainly for my nose. I just pull my shirt sleeves down if it's too hot.'

I felt John was quite open and honest with me about his

scrounging. He had no problem with it, it was just part of life and how he survived. It was John. Simple, uncomplicated and living as he wanted. Whether he told me all – I doubt it, I'm sure there was more to this man that I could have learnt, but he had some more miles to travel and so did I.

John was packed and we shook hands firmly. 'It's been an experience, thanks, Allan,' he said. I handed him $20, and wished it was more. Had I been near a bank it would have been. I promised him I'd get a copy of the book to him. He gave me the address of some friends he calls on near Gravesend, and I said to make sure he gets it. I hoped we'd meet again on the road somewhere, as we are both constant travellers.

He had all his possessions on his back and draped across a shoulder and arm, a silver mug dangling from a strap. We shook hands firmly and I wished him a safe journey. He headed off north towards Echuca, as I prepared to leave. I took some more photos as he left and had a sad feeling. I wanted to do more for the man, but I respected his wishes to remain a free spirit and watched him leave. His load looked heavy as he trudged along in the rubber-soled shoes that he'd found some-where along the road. His homemade bags of possessions looked to envelop him, and strangely somehow his arms looked extra long with the weight on his back. I watched him go.

It felt almost obscene for me to be driving a Ford F250 with lots and lots of extras and worth over $80,000, loaded with bags of possessions, laptop computer, mobile phone and more. In the back was a large comfortable swag, which I use less these days. But far too large for John to carry so I don't think he would have accepted it anyway. I look around the ute to see what else I could give him.

As I drove off I switched the air-conditioner on, but the radio off. One last look in the rear view mirror and John was but a diminishing shadow on the distant horizon as I sat back in comfort to let the cruise control on the ute do its job.

Soon I was lost in my own thoughts. For me too, John, it had been quite an experience, and I thank you for your time. It was good to spend time under a gumtree in the Australian bush with a free spirit. Travel safe, mate.

THE OTHER SIDE TO JOHN'S STORY . . .
They say all things happen for a reason.

Was I supposed to come into John's life? I don't know. But I did and I had a feeling I couldn't just leave it at that, there was something more I needed to do. It was a nagging feeling. I knew that his family would still want to know about John after all these years. I was concerned, however – I felt an obligation to John and didn't want to cause him any drama and I determined I would respect his wishes. He did, however, say if I ever spoke to his brother then it was okay.

During our interview I had asked John about family, without wanting to push the issue too much. He said, 'My parents – they'd be dead by now, I think.' I asked very little about it as I felt I had intruded. Did he have any other family? He said he had a brother: 'He was still at school when I left, he'd be 38 now, a big difference in our ages.' As it was obvious there were many memories for John I changed the subject for a while and we spoke of other things.

It was then that I told John how a lady contacted me years ago after a photo of her father appeared in one of my books, the father she never knew. I asked if his brother contacted me when the book was published, what would he want me to say. 'It'd be good if I saw him, but I'd never want to impose on him, but if we did meet well and good but if not that's okay.' John gave me his name and I said I would pass on his thoughts if I ever met his brother. John looked pensive when we talked of family, and I sensed a loss. I determined in my own mind that I would try and locate his brother.

John's surname is an unusual name of French origin, so I hoped I might track his family down. When I arrived home that night I searched the White Pages briefly before bed, but Bruce's family name didn't appear to be listed. The next day, however, I decided to check country Victoria, particularly Minyip. Although no one with his surname appeared there, I did find one listed at Horsham and one at Ballarat. First I rang the Horsham number. An elderly woman answered the phone and I asked if she could help me. I was trying to locate a Bruce by the same surname as her. 'Bruce is my son,' she said, 'he lives in Melbourne.' I asked if she had another son and before I could say it, she said, 'Yes, Grant John.' There was an urgency and expectation in her voice.

It was John's mother.

I told her I'd found him and told her he was well. She was so excited and said they'd been looking for him for over twenty-five years. She was very flustered and overwhelmed. We talked and shared some time and I knew I'd made an old lady very happy. She mentioned her daughter and that she wanted to tell her. I told her I'd let her ring and I'd be in touch.

Shortly afterwards my phone rang and it was John's sister Michelle. She was even more excited than her mother. We talked for a long while and I was able to tell her much of John and what he's been doing and how he lives. She said all the family just want to see him. She says no one minds how he lives, they just want to see him again. She said he sent a couple of letters and a couple of Christmas cards to them over the years indicating that he didn't want to impose on them. They are just so happy he is alive and well, and desperately want to see him. I told her I would try and catch up with him and pass on their thoughts and details. She said her father now lives in Caloundra and at 82 is desperate to see his son before he dies.

The family have never stopped searching for John. Whenever they got a card they would write to the post office where the card had been posted and ask if anyone knew him. They sent posters out. They had him listed on missing persons lists. And the Salvation Army have been trying to locate him. But nothing. A couple of cards since 1996, but no card last year. They knew that John now felt he didn't belong. But he does. Michelle said they have never stopped loving him and she asked me to give him a big hug and a kiss. I said she could do that herself; I'd shake his hand.

I was now determined to reunite this family, either by him going to them or them going to him. 'We don't care, we'd just love to see him,' said Michelle enthusiastically. 'We'll go to his territory if need be. Anywhere. We'd give anything to catch up with him again.'

I promised Michelle I would try and track him down again.

The next day I headed off again in the vain hope I might find him. I wasn't sure: I wondered if he had had second thoughts and gone in a different direction so he couldn't be found. By the time I got to where we last met he would probably be at least 60 kilometres further away in any direction. But

I needed to let him know what I had discovered.

It was a long shot but I also had some determination and the 'detective' in me started to kick in. I really wanted to find him and tell him. It would be up to him what he did then – I wasn't going to force him but at least I now had a page of names, addresses and phone numbers to give him if he did feel he'd like to contact his family again. My role would then be done.

I searched some roads between Echuca and in the general direction of Shepparton, as he said that was where he would head. The day wore on and no luck, and I backtracked my way to and around Echuca, before taking other roads. Finally, I stopped at the Falcon hotel on the road east of town. As I walked towards the door, I noticed a food delivery van pull up. 'Wouldn't have seen a bloke about 50 carrying a swag and gear on the road, would you, mate?'

'Yeah, he's on the road towards Tongala, I just saw him.' The man gave me directions which road to go. 'He's about five kilometres down that road.' I thanked him and he said no worries. Now I knew now I'd find him. I went into the pub and ordered a beer. I also ordered a sandwich for John.

Shortly after I was heading down the right road and before long I spotted him. I pulled up, and told him I had something to tell him. Let's sit in the shade, I said, so he walked to a fence and sat down relieving himself of his bags. 'Thought you might like a turkey and salad sandwich, mate,' I said as I handed it to him. He immediately started to unwrap it.

John was very quiet when I explained all the news of his family. I could tell he was rather shocked by it all. He looked off into the distant paddock. A large bull was at the fence opposite us, calling out a mournful sound. John was quiet. I could tell, though, he was very interested. We talked for a while and I let it all sink in. Finally I asked, 'So, what do you think of that, John?'

He looked at me with those penetrating blue eyes. 'I think I need time to think it all over,' he replied. It was all a big shock.

When I assured John there was no pressure on him from the family and they just wanted to see him – either he come to them or they'd come to 'his territory' just to say hello – he seemed both keen and unsure.

'John, I'll make you an offer. We can throw your gear in the ute, and I'll drive you to either Horsham or Ballarat and you can see your mum or your sister. Or if you prefer, they could come and meet you somewhere. I'll do whatever you want.'

He listened and looked off into the distance. I knew it was a big day in John's life. It all had to be his decision. I offered to come back the next day if he wanted; I'd go and stay in Echuca. But he already had things ticking over in his mind. I handed him the sheet of paper with the contact details of his various family members. He read it over and over and over in silence.

Eventually he said, 'I could ring Michelle from Shepparton, and when I work it out I could meet her somewhere.' He was trying to work out how long it would take to get there, and when he could ring her, and where they'd meet. I told him whatever suited him, would suit them. I think he wanted to remain on his territory and where he was comfortable, but the urge to see them all again was obviously very much there.

Finally I got ready to leave. I knew I needed to leave him alone with his thoughts. I promised him I'd let Michelle know he would ring her. He now was pretty sure in his mind. He stood by the door of my ute all loaded up. I handed him $10 to ring home. He thanked me a number of times for my help.

As I went to do a u-turn to head back towards Echuca John said, 'When your book is published, perhaps you could send it to Michelle – if I'm going to keep in touch with her now, she could get it to me.'

I was thrilled. John must have made the decision that a family reunion was at hand. I assured him I would. He plodded off and I headed for Echuca to ring Michelle, as my mobile was out of range. Michelle said she'd meet him near Nagambie as he suggested. She'd wait by the phone to hear from him. She was excited. I had asked him did he want to see them all or just Michelle, and he said it was okay for all to come. He would tell her on the phone directions on how to get to a small rest stop near Nagambie. I told Michelle I would again go back out to find John and let him know. So off I went again. This time John had just passed through the town of Tongala and was on the edge of town, walking. Again I told him the news and he agreed he would get to Shepparton in the next couple of days and ring her.

And so we parted company again. It was a few hours' drive home for me. En route, though, I knew there was something I had to do. I collected some photos from home that I'd had printed of John. I rang Michelle. 'Will you be home this afternoon?' I said. Michelle was excited. 'Yes, I sure will, and so will Mum, she arrived from Horsham and is here with me now.'

A couple of hours later and I was on the doorstep in Ballarat. Michelle threw her arms around me in a big hug. Soon we were seated at the kitchen table. Michelle, her mother June and myself.

I knew immediately what they needed. 'I won't keep you in suspense,' I said as I put some photos of John on the table. June and Michelle looked intently and eagerly at the pictures.

Neither of the women said they recognised him.

'I would have walked past him in the street and not even known it was him,' said his mother, and Michelle agreed. They looked long and intently.

They showed me a couple of photos of what he was like at his twenty-first birthday and another a couple of years before he had left. Then he wore thick black glasses and was quite heavy. 'We get better looking as we get older,' said Michelle. Looking at the photos I agreed he had changed dramatically.

In order for June and Michelle to know of John's life, I read out twelve pages of his story as I had already written it in first rough draft form. I felt it would answer some questions and detail what his life was. They listened intently. I could tell June was overwhelmed and she questioned me quite a bit. I think she needed to know in her own mind that it really was her son. She looked down at the table a lot. Michelle was enthusiastic. She had a file with his few letters and cards, a file that also included copies of the missing persons reports, newspaper clippings, etc. – all about their loved one.

'We never stopped loving him, you know,' said Michelle.

I told them the importance of this story is to help tell other families who might be in the same situation as them, to give them hope about their own lost loved ones, and that I would like to pass on their side of the story. They agreed.

June and Michelle told me much the same as John had, and that he worked in a bank and just left.

'We just never understood why,' said June. 'He graduated from school, passing all his exams. He then chose to go into the bank to work. Finally, years later, he came to us one day and said he was leaving, and that some of his possessions, like all his books, he just gave to his flatmates. All he wanted to do was get to Perth.

'He left from Geelong where his mates were staying. I think he had some interest in a girl, and I remember asking would he marry her. He replied, "Oh Mum, she wouldn't want to marry me." Anyway, off he went. He didn't know what work he would do, he just wanted to go off hitchhiking. It wasn't long afterwards that I left his father and we divorced. It was about November 1977. We expected to hear from him at Christmas. And we never heard from him again, until the letter in August 1996.'

June kept saying how she didn't understand. 'He wasn't close to his father, he was always very quiet and a deep thinker, always loved reading. Him and I were very close.'

Michelle related about the last time she saw him, not far from where she was living now. There was so much they related, but foremost was his disappearance, and why. I asked how it affected them. 'It left a bloody big hole,' said June.

'My words exactly,' Michelle immediately added.

'I just cried and cried for years. If you knew what I've gone through,' said June. 'I used to cry at night. We were very close. His little brother Bruce looked up to him. He idolised him.'

'It really broke Mum's heart,' said Michelle. 'She was a real wreck for about the first five years.'

I asked if they ever gave up hope. 'There was a period when Mum did. She felt something must have happened to him.'

'I thought something might have happened at Geelong. I just didn't know.'

What was the worst about it all? 'Not knowing, just not knowing if he was alive or not,' replied June, and Michelle agreed.

'We never stopped searching, you know,' said June. 'I had to wait for six months before they'd consider him a "missing person". We had police looking, and the Salvation Army did a search. We put ads in papers. Even when Bruce got married we put it in in case he read it, just to let him know.'

The family also searched every phone book and went through the electoral rolls.

I asked did they ever think he may have just married and blended in to a new life somewhere. 'No not really, just felt something must have happened,' said June.

The family have had people tell them they'd seen him over the years. Michelle said, 'They reckon they saw him in Melbourne, but we don't think he would ever go back there. Then others said they'd seen him around, but who knows.'

June said, 'I still have people ask me if I've found my son. All the people in Horsham and Minyip and other people I know often ask.'

So how do they feel now after all these years?

'Overwhelmed. I just don't know, I guess it hasn't hit me properly yet. I know I'm relieved. Relieved. There's a bit of sadness and happiness at the same time. I don't think he could ever come back now, he'd find it hard after all these years. He'd have to get a job, and I think he'd probably find it different from the way he's been living,' June replied. Michelle is just happy he's been found.

We discussed many aspects of John's life and I told them more of how I felt about his situation, hoping that they would just take it as it comes, and realise it from his point of view as well. There is a big gap in this family, but I think the time was right. It was meant to happen. What has been in the past is just that – it's the past, and it can't be changed.

As recently as last month details of John appeared in the Salvation Army's *War Cry* magazine. The family, as recently as six months ago, went to the Salvation Army to start a new search for him.

'It was all because of Dad,' said Michelle. 'He's 82, and had some heart problem. He lives in Caloundra, Queensland, now, and I stay in touch with him. He said to me one day all he wanted to do before he dies is to see his son again. And so we paid for a new search to be done by the Salvos. It only cost $40.

'Recently Dad said to me, "Do you think if I paid more money to them, they'd try even harder?" As soon as Dad heard we'd found him, he wanted to get onto an aeroplane and come down, but he goes into hospital this Wednesday to have some sun cancers taken off. He is so happy he's been found.'

It's interesting to see how a family clings on to hope. Michelle relates a story that shows hope. 'Before he left home, my brother had a book about the Hare Krishnas. Many years later Dad (also John) saw an ad in the paper, that there was an open day at the Hare Krishna commune in Queensland near where he now lives. So Dad went there, and the whole day he just walked up and down looking at people, hoping to see his son.'

And for one of John's nephews who he had never met, it is also good news. One of Michelle's children, who is in Melbourne, said to his mother, 'Great, I'm going to meet my uncle.' Happy also is brother Bruce, who is pretty overwhelmed by it all as well. I guess in times like these when the family is so close yet still away from their lost one, it is understandable to want to do something. 'Yesterday, Bruce just walked past the bank where his brother used to work, just to see it again.'

And what would they say to any other families who read this who have someone missing?

June: 'Never give up.'

Michelle: 'My very words.'

Never give up.

Finally I had to leave them. June gave me a hug and put her head on my shoulder. 'Don't worry, it'll all work out,' was all I could say. Michelle again hugged me. All I could do now was wait, like them, to hear that John had rung, and the private family reunion took place somewhere in John's territory.

I have seen John again, and his mother and sister have been reunited with him twice in country towns. The second time his brother also spent time with him. Some six-and-a-half hours each time, just talking and sharing food in a park. The family is coming together again and it thrills me to bits.

In early January, Michelle rang me to inform me John had sent a beautiful Christmas card and letter to his mother, and has also since written to his father. Later I received word that John and his father had been reunited. As I write this, John is staying at his dad's place for a while before he heads south to visit his mother and then his sister, brother, nieces, nephews and cousins.

The final positive note in this story is that John said in a letter to his family that he felt that '2003 will be a good year for all of us.'

Postscript

John now writes a daily diary which he sends to his family once a month. He remains in touch and now travels from one family member to another. He maintains his free lifestyle – but now has more purpose in choosing his destinations. Travel safe and good luck, mate.

Grandma's Kitchen

GRACE NIXON

'NOTHING SO GRAND AS A COUNTRY KITCHEN.'

There would be few places in a home that are so evocative as the kitchen, and never more so than the kitchen of a home in the bush. It is the place where swaggies would come, past the Coolgardie safe swinging on the verandah, to ask the cocky's wife for their daily needs of flour, sugar and tea. Where the ice cart pulled up to deliver its refreshing cargo. Where the house dogs scratched the door and whined for a morsel from the Sunday roast.

Many of the interviews that form this book took place in kitchens across the country. Many a cuppa was downed as today's bushies shared their lives and stories with me. Clearly, the kitchen is still the hub of the home paddock.

The kitchen is the heart of a home, where life and memories are constant. In my case, my grandma's country kitchen holds wonderful memories, and I'm sure readers who reflect will have their own memories also. But this story is a tribute to a lady. She was the housewife, the homemaker; she was mother, grandmother and great grandmother. She was Grace Nixon.

We should all stop and think of those that went before us. Take your time to remember yours. This is mine. This is my tribute to Grandma.

I remember Grandma's kitchen on those cold winter days, those wonderful smells at dinnertime on Saturday. I often lit the fire on that wondrous big stove. It was all black with lots of silver trimming on the two oven doors, the knobs all kept polished, the stove itself blackened with black lead. I also remember the whistling fountain filled with water, with its shiny brass tap.

I'd cut the kindling in the woodshed and bring in logs for the wood box on the hearth. It had a lift-up lid and vinyl-padded seat to sit on. One match was all it took as the daily newspaper began to burn and the small kindling crackled. I loved the way that first whiff of smoke always found its way to my eyes and nose.

The rain drummed its even pattern on the shiny corrugated iron roof. Grandma would be at the table humming, her lovely apron covering her dress. On the rough wooden table were spread her tools of trade – large china bowl for the ingredients, wooden spoon for mixing and the flour sifter. In another bowl, a glass one, were a few eggs, straight from the chook pen. Grandma knew what she was doing; she had done it all before.

I got to stir the mixture, and afterwards clean the bowl and lick the contents off the wooden spoon! She interrupted her humming and softly told me that there was no need to mix it so fast, but to gently fold it and blend it smooth. She would place her warm wrinkled hand on mine and we would work the mixture together.

Finally the oven would be ready, its temperature was just right – I don't know how she knew, but she'd just thrust her hand into the oven to test it, pull it out and quickly close the door. Time to lay the creamy yellow dough into a round tin baking dish with the hole in the middle. First, though, Grandma would grease the inside with butter, using greaseproof paper rolled into a ball. In went the mixture. She'd smooth it all round, then into the oven it went. I'd watch in silent awe. But the best was still to come.

We'd fill in time, while it slowly cooked. The table had to be cleaned, the dishes washed – and still the rain would fall in ever-deafening patter. Grandma's humming continued, the old clock on the mantle chimed.

Finally with a tea towel she'd carefully remove the tin dish from the oven and place it on the wire rack on the table – all golden brown. A wonderful steamy aroma filled the room. Tipped upside down it fell from the tin and then she'd tip it right side up again. With a small brush she'd glaze the top of the cake with a beaten egg. Then came the best part – the cinnamon packet from the cupboard. Grandma would spread an even amount all over and top it off with sugar too. How I remember Grandma's teacake!

I've grown to manhood now – no longer do we make our teacake, Grandma and me. Now our cakes come in plastic bags from the supermarkets, but they never taste the same. The rain still patters down on the corrugated iron, but now the roof – well, it's rusty and it leaks.

The kitchen hasn't altered – all the items are still there, but there's a different feeling now. The clock no longer chimes – it's long worn out. The spiderwebs are thick where once they would never be seen. And that wonderful wood stove, it's long gone cold. No longer will the firebox hold embers – it's all gone rusty, and the wood box is empty.

Grandma doesn't remember how to make those cakes now; maybe I'll make one for her. Her days are spent in the sunroom – her quiet and peaceful abode. Her feeble withered hands are no longer able to command, her knitting needles lie silent, her mind is silent too.

Who knows what she is thinking? Maybe she really does remember those days. I'll always remember them – our lovely rainy Saturdays – and Grandma's kitchen.

Grandma's Teacake

Put one cup self-raising flour,
½ cup sugar, ½ cup milk,
1 tablespoon butter,
½ teaspoon vanilla,
1 egg
into a basin, beat together and bake in oven in sandwich tin for
about 25 minutes at 375 degrees Fahrenheit.
After it's cooked, sprinkle cinnamon and sugar on top.

Postscript

Not long after writing the above tribute to Grandma, I bought the teacake ingredients and drove to see her. She was in her sunroom as usual, and I told her I was going to make a teacake just as she had taught me all those years ago. She was pleased and said she hadn't had one for such a long time. She didn't think she'd know how to make one now.

We had a great time. A cup of tea and our teacake together in the sunroom just yarning and talking of the 'good old days'. She loved it and although I felt a great warmth I also had a sad feeling. She was slipping away before my eyes and I couldn't do a thing about it.

But I knew that it was a part of life, and sometimes we just have to let go. I wanted this day, though, just her and me. Something was completed between us, a gentle peace, unspoken words, and understanding, a final bond. It happened that day.

Finally I kissed her goodbye as usual, and went to leave. Then I stopped and placed my hand on her shoulder. I found it hard to say the words – I don't remember having said them before – but I knew I wanted to say them now. I turned and said, 'I love you, Grandma.' Without hesitation, she softly replied, 'And I love you.' I had a lump in my throat.

We would never share a teacake again.

It was not long after that she died, and life was never quite the same. In her passing went an era. As long as I knew her she only had one kitchen, and for me it was a refuge. It never changed in all my life, and when she went I never went back, never saw it again. I didn't want to, as I needed to remember it, and that old kitchen clock is now on my mantle. Just a reminder as it was, when it was in Grandma's kitchen.